Plain Beautiful:
The Life of Peggy Ann Garner

by

Sandra Grabman

Foreword by Margaret O'Brien

Plain Beautiful:

The Life of Peggy Ann Garner

by

Sandra Grabman

Foreword by Margaret O'Brien

BearManor Media
2005

Plain Beautiful: The Life of Peggy Ann Garner
© 2005 Sandra Grabman
Foreword © 2005 Margaret O'Brien

For information, address:

BearManor Media
P. O. Box 750
Boalsburg, PA 16827

bearmanormedia.com

Cover photo by Jeff Howard
Cover design by John Teehan
Typesetting and layout by John Teehan

Published in the USA by BearManor Media

Library of Congress Cataloging-in-Publication Data

Grabman, Sandra.
Plain beautiful : the life of Peggy Ann Garner / by Sandra
Grabman; foreword by Margaret O'Brien.
p. cm.
Includes index.
ISBN 1-59393-017-8
1. Garner, Peggy Ann. 2. Motion picture actors and
actresses--United States--Biography. I. Title.

PN2287.G387G73 2005
791.4302'8'092--dc22
2005001837

ISBN—1-59393-017-8

DEDICATION

This book is dedicated to two wonderful people who were instrumental in making it a reality:

To Peggy Ann's best friend, Barbara Whiting Smith, who graciously shared many happy and touching memories. Their adult lives went in very different directions, but the two ladies remained close to the end.

And, to my hard-working research assistant, actor/producer Jeff Howard. He put much thought and long hours into helping me get all the information I needed to put this book together. He's also the one who took the photo you see on the cover. Profuse thanks weren't necessary; his admiration for Peggy Ann was all the incentive he needed.

TABLE OF CONTENTS

Acknowledgements

Many, many thanks to all the people who have so graciously shared their memories with me or helped in the research of this book:

Information and Assistance:
Elizabeth B. Anthony, "B," Ruth Bricker, Kurt Brown, Mary Calvert, Michael Elliott, Celia Foster, Jenna Girard, Klaus D. Haisch, Lelisia Hall, Elaine Hill, Katherine Hersch, Jerome A. Holst, Ed Jenkins, Jo LaJoie, James Laperouse, Nancy Paajanen, Emily Peters, Lizanne Salmi, Ron Schultz, Michael Schwibs, Laurie Slavin, Laura Wagner, Yvonne Whiteley, and Marie Wiorski

Peggy's Relatives:
Vince DeVito, Jr., Vince DeVito, Sr., Mary Eckard, Betty Muse Eschliman, letters of Catherine Ann Salmi, Connie Stratton, the estate of Virginia Garner Swainston, and Marilyn Muse Wolf

Contributing Co-Stars and Others in the Entertainment Industry:
Carol Burnett, Del Courtney, Nina Foch, Joan Fontaine, Richard Hayes, Pat Hingle, Earl Holliman, Sybil Jason, Lon McCallister, Rod McKuen, Randal Malone, Rose Marie, Dina Merrill, Dick Moore, Richard Ney, Margaret O'Brien, Gregory Peck, Rex Reed, Peter Mark Richman, the memoirs of Albert Salmi, Johnny Sheffield, Elizabeth Taylor, and Barbara Whiting Smith

Research Assistance:
The Academy of Motion Pictures Arts and Sciences, Michael Escarzaga, Jenna Girard, Mike Needs, Jeff Howard, and Ron Schultz

Finnish Interpreter:
  Nancy Paajanen

Publications:
  The Akron Beacon Journal, Family Circle, Films in Review, Films of the Golden Age, Inside TV, Life, Miss America, Modern Screen, Motion Picture, Movie Life, Movie News, Movie Stars Parade, Movie Teen, New Dynamo, Photoplay, Picture Goer, Quick, The [Canton] Repository, Rexall, Screen Greats, Screen Guide, Screen Stars, Screenland, Siirtokansan Kalenteri, TV Fan, TV Radio Mirror, and *TV Show*

Photos:
  Philo Barnhart, Mary Eckard, Michael Escarzaga, the estate of Ina Bernstein Sharr, the DeVito family, Florence Doyle, Jim Holman, Jeff Howard, Sybil Jason, Peter Kasimatis, Roddy McDowall/Virginia McDowall, New York Public Library, Margaret O'Brien, Mary O'Hara, Ron Schultz, Johnny Sheffield, Connie Stratton, The Stumpf-Ohmart Collection, the estate of Virginia Swainston, and Laura Wagner

Cover Photo:
  Jeff Howard

Fan Contributions (chapbook):
  Dottie B., Scott Delcoco, Ann L. Feldmann, Warren F. Hall, Jeff Howard, Louise Parshall, Emily Peters, Ron Schultz, Robert Sivanich, Bruce Steller, Gary R. Thomas, and Jane Ward

Editorial Assistance:
  Ben Ohmart

FOREWORD

The first thing that comes to my mind today when I hear Peggy Ann Garner's name is what an amazing little actress she was. Her work in such wonderful films as *A Tree Grows in Brooklyn* will live on forever. This is the kind of rich legacy she left us.

I was fortunate to have worked with Peggy on numerous projects over the years and to have gotten to know her as a dear friend. As children, we didn't have a lot of opportunity to socialize because I was under contract at MGM, and Peggy was at Fox. However, when we would run into each other at a special event or Hollywood function, she would always come over and greet me very warmly. Peggy was the type of girl that, even if you haven't seen each other for a while, she remained your friend. She was genuine.

But every now and then, I would catch a glimpse of it—a certain look in her eyes. Was it sadness? Loneliness? Yearning? I was never quite sure what was behind that haunting look, but her life story, documented in this book, sheds some light on that. Peggy experienced many sorrows and joys but, throughout them all, she always remained the same sweet, caring lady she had always been. One couldn't ask for a better friend.

She was just plain beautiful.

Margaret O'Brien
2004

Introduction

This biography is centered around the beloved, Oscar-winning child star of the 1940s, Peggy Ann Garner. In order to tell the whole story, however, we must understand two other women in her life as well. The lives of Peggy, her mother, Virginia, and Peggy's daughter, Catherine, were intricately interwoven. The strong-willed matriarch at the beginning of their story is the last woman left as it ends. She had taken extreme measures to do what she thought was best, but it had resulted in pain and estrangement.

From letters, documents, and photographs gleaned from Virginia Garner Swainston's estate, we see her side of the story in detail. It looked much different, however, from Peggy's perspective, and different still from Catherine's.

Peggy Ann Garner has been admired by filmgoers and historians for decades. To the young girl of the 1940s who felt shunted aside in favor of the prettier child, she was a heroine and role model. To adults of that era, she was the daughter they wish they had. Even to cinema lovers who were born too late to see her first-run films in the theaters, she is awesome. Peggy won awards for her work, including a very special Oscar when she was only thirteen.

Even death couldn't separate Peggy from her admirers. Five years after her passing, *Hollywood Studio Magazine* included in their Bathing Beauty Quiz a photo of the bubbly, teenaged Peggy climbing out of a pool while flashing a joyful smile at her friends. Two years later, Alex Gonzales copyrighted a set of Peggy Ann Garner paperdolls, featuring fashions she had worn in the films of her youth. To this day, her friends are fiercely protective of her memory.

Peggy Ann Garner left a permanent imprint on everyone she met. Let's tap the memories of her friends, co-stars, and relatives and find out why.

NOTE

One important source of information for this book was letters—those written by Peggy Ann, her daughter Catherine, and her mother Virginia. Of these letter-writers, Virginia was by far the most prolific. Excerpts from her March 4, 1959 letter to Judge DeMatteis explaining, in detail, the happenings of the previous eleven years, are set in bold print.

Not only was Virginia prolific, but she was also boldly accusatory. Therefore, portions of this letter had to be censored—the name of Peggy's agent and his agency have been changed in order to protect innocent parties.

CHAPTER 1

There was nothing plain about Peggy Ann Garner. Sure, the studio's publicity department promoted her as such, and her mother wouldn't allow little Peggy to show up at auditions with makeup or ornamentation of any kind, but the child's plainness was just as contrived as a sex kitten's beauty is. After all, her mother reasoned, Hollywood was already deluged with Shirley Temple wannabes. Beautiful children were everywhere. But present a child as the simple friend, whose plainness made the star look even better, and her chances of being cast in a motion picture improved dramatically.

Virginia Garner was an incredibly clever woman. When it came to her little girl, no one had more drive and ambition than she.

Originally from Spennymoor, England, William George Huxley Warburton Garner immigrated to Canton, Ohio, with his parents and sister Catherine in September of 1920.

Virginia Jeane Craig had grown up with sister Helen and brother Karl. Their parents were good, caring people who could be counted on to go the extra mile for their children.

On April 7, 1931, twenty-six-year-old Bill and nineteen-year-old Virginia married in Toledo, Ohio. They made their home at 1102 Market Avenue NW in Canton. He was an attorney-at-law, working for a mortgage company, so their future looked secure.

Ten months later, Virginia gave birth to a daughter. Little Peggy Ann Garner had arrived at 9:40 a.m. on February 3, 1932, at the nearby Aultmann Hospital. Of this Virginia was adamant: She wanted her daughter's proper name to be Peggy, not Margaret.

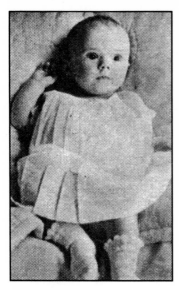

Baby Peggy Ann Garner. [From the collection of Jeff Howard]

The country was in the midst of the Great Depression at that time, and Bill had lost his job. He realized he had to do something quickly so he could support his family. A job was offered to him in Washington, D.C., as a legal adviser to the British Embassy. It was a good job, very prestigious, but did not pay well. These were hard times, though, so he knew he had better accept it. The family then moved to Washington.

Peggy was the apple of her parents' eye. She was never physically punished. If she misbehaved, it would not result in a spanking or even a slap. Virginia's method of discipline was to reason with her instead.

The young mother had big plans for her child's future. Before marrying Bill, Virginia had attended Greenbrier College. Now, she enrolled her little girl in the same college—much in advance, of course. Peggy was enrolled for the year of 1950, or thereabouts.

There are several versions of how the chain of events that led to Peggy's career began. This is the one seen most often: Virginia took Peggy for a visit to her parents' home in New Jersey. Peggy was to begin kindergarten soon and Grandma Craig wanted to buy her some pretty, new clothes, so they

Peggy was born at Aultman Hospital in Canton, Ohio.

took her to a store in New York City. As she was trying an outfit on and looking at herself in the full-length mirror, they were approached by a handsome man who asked, "Is your little girl a professional model?"

"Professional? Why no."

"Well, she should be," he said. He then gave them his card. He was John Robert Powers, the man who owned the modeling agency that had provided so many attractive models for advertisements. "If you'd like to

Baby Peggy Ann Garner.

consider the profession for her, look me up," he said. "Her face is expressive. She speaks, without words, through her eyes."

Virginia recognized opportunity when she saw it and soon got representation for their daughter with Powers' modeling agency. After all, she thought, the Great Depression might have wiped out money they would have saved for Peggy's college education, but modeling paid well. She could build the child's college savings with modeling money. Through the Powers agency, Peggy was given her first professional job, that of a pint-sized fashion model for newsreels.

The modeling instructor suggested that Peggy be given dancing les-

Daddy's little girl (From the collection of Jeff Howard)

The little model with her Grandmas Garner and Craig.
(From the collection of Connie Stratton)

sons to increase her poise and balance, so Virginia arranged for her little prodigy to take lessons at the Marion Venable Dancing School. At first, she was stunned by the cost. The school's head watched Peggy dance a bit and agreed to give the Garners a much lower fee. They accepted.

Now it was the dancing instructor who came back with yet another suggestion—acting lessons. She knew just the right place to get them— the Alviene School of the Drama in New York City. Virginia followed up

Portrait of Peggy Ann Garner (From the collection of Connie Stratton)

and found that this school charged what appeared to her to be an exorbitant fee. After being shown the child and told about the family's financial plight, they also agreed to lower their price.

Even with the reduced costs for these valuable lessons, the Garners' expenses were still more than their income. Virginia then sought a job for herself to help supplement Bill's income. It had to be night work, though, so she'd be free to take Peggy to her various appointments during the day. Thus, she got a job in the Personnel Department of the New Yorker Hotel while her parents babysat Peggy.

For her first stage role, *Mrs. Wiggs of the Cabbage Patch*, at the Olney Theatre, five-year-old Peggy had the distinction of being the youngest member of their summer stock company. The company presented the play in both New York and Washington. So impressed were people by Peggy's acting talent that they urged Virginia to take her to Hollywood and get her into the movies. Maybe she could be another Shirley Temple, they thought. Virginia was more realistic. Only a fool would try to be a carbon copy of Shirley, America's little sweetheart, so she knew better than to go that route; but there *was* opportunity aplenty for children to play supporting roles. These parts would most likely be given to less-attractive actors, however, so she scrubbed her daughter's face and carefully combed her straight blonde hair, and off to Hollywood they went. It was October of 1938; Peggy was now six.

Virginia took with her a letter of introduction to Dave Chasen, the manager of one of Hollywood's ritziest restaurants. Both Chasen and Virginia called upon casting directors, one after another.

Stubborn persistence is what it took, and that's what Virginia had in abundance. Any rejections she experienced just made her more determined. It was through Virginia's cleverness and, yes, maybe just a bit of deceit, that got her into the inner sanctums of the casting directors. The Vice President of the United States was named John Nance Garner. Hoping they would assume she was the wife of this man, rather than Bill Garner, Virginia would call and say, "This is Mrs. Garner of Washington, D.C. I wonder if I might come out to see you." It worked! Once she got in, she showed them Peggy Ann.

Little did Virginia know the years of heartache that awaited her.

CHAPTER 2

It wasn't easy getting Peggy into movies, but Virginia's flamboyance and determination, plus the intentional unadorned plainness of her daughter, would eventually make her dream a reality. Peggy was the first normal-looking child the casting directors had seen in ages, and they remembered that. Virginia and Peggy were in town for only five weeks when director John Farrow gave Peggy a screen test, then awarded her with a small part at Warner Brothers. The film was called *Little Miss Thoroughbred*, and starred Ann Sheridan. Peggy received twenty-five dollars for her small part, then there was a dry spell for about eighteen months.

While awaiting other opportunities, Peggy attended Selma Avenue School in Los Angeles, where she made a new friend.

"Peggy and I were best friends and neighbors when she and her mother came to Hollywood," says Ruth Bricker. "Peggy and I played with two other girls up the street, and we spent a lot of time creating plays, playing jacks, hopscotch, monopoly and giggling." They roller-skated too, "but the most fun was getting the other kids together and putting on plays. There were a lot of plays that I can remember that Peggy played the queen or the princess (always, a tiara)," Ruth says. Perhaps Peggy wanted to play such glamorous roles in order to reassure herself that she was, indeed, attractive. "Even at those delicate ages," Ruth continues, "we had the Hollywood lingo in operation during these productions—the director, producer, star (Peggy) and even the character and bit players, as well as the extras. You might recall that *Gone With the Wind* had a huge impact on all of us at any age. We all had seen the movie and were very taken with the drama and the costumes. Peggy and friends spent hours with the 'cut

School days.

outs' that were published at the time. A lot of the plays did try for some of the GWTW effect. I even remember Peggy trying out the Scarlett behavior and southern accent."

Peggy was a smart little girl and brought home good grades on her report card. "We would often walk together [to school]," Ruth continues, "since I passed by her apartment on the way. I recall another girl who lived in her apartment house named Drucilla. She was older than I—and both Peggy and I adored her. At nine, she was quoting Shakespeare."

At least one of their classmates was destined for greatness: "When [Peggy] was at Selma, it was at a time when a few kids who were able to get out of Germany enrolled. One of those kids was André Previn. His uncle was musical director at MGM studios and it was already clear that he was a prodigy. However, that didn't stop us (all the kids) from making fun of him. He talked funny, he wore short pants (all the other boys wore what would pass for jeans today) and he played the piano. The school held weekly 'auds' for special programs in the auditorium that the entire school would attend. There were a number of performers at the school, but Andre was chosen to play every week. Unfortunately, the only piece he knew by heart was 'Clare de Lune.'"

Peggy's adjustment to her new environment was interrupted on January 9, 1939, when her mother was arrested by the Los Angeles police for seven counts of fictitious checks. Virginia, of course, wasn't able to take care of Peggy while in jail, so her mother came out to California. Virginia was released on bond on January 27. When it was time to face the judge, she pled guilty to two counts, and the others were dismissed.

Another small role was offered to Peggy in a film called *In Name Only* for R.K.O. studios. She was to play leading lady Carole Lombard's daughter. The little trooper did her part and did it well.

In March, Virginia was served papers that her husband, who had remained back east, had filed for divorce. He charged her with gross neglect of duty. His petition said that Virginia had made numerous trips to

A cover girl already, on *Movie Story Magazine*, featuring *In Name Only.*

Chicago, New York, and Los Angeles, taking Peggy with her without his consent. He also cited her entanglements with the law due to the passing of bad checks, and the fact that he had been forced to cover those checks himself. As an attorney now for the Federal Surplus Commodities Corporation, Virginia's behavior was putting his career in a precarious position.

"No problem," thought Virginia. Without a husband to deal with, she could now concentrate fully on Peggy's career. Virginia agreed not to contest the divorce and thought no more about it. Bill had asked the court for custody of seven-year-old Peggy, allowing her to live with his

With Carole Lombard and Kay Francis in *In Name Only*.
(From the collection of Connie Stratton)

mother when she wasn't needed in Hollywood. His request for custody
was denied.

It was Virginia's understanding that Bill would continue to support
not only Peggy, but her as well.

Virginia might have had little use for Bill, but their daughter certainly felt differently. She missed her daddy terribly. "Peggy had a lot of
sadness about her," says one of her friends. "It was a tragedy in Peggy's life,
I believe, to be taken away [from her father] like that." To help deal with
her sadness, Peggy would cuddle her tiny stuffed animals.

"[I] realized that she was essentially a homeless child when she wasn't
at the studio working," says Ruth Bricker. "Unfortunately, her mother,
Virginia, was not only the typical, tough 'movie mother,' but she also had
a drinking problem. Often, she would lock Peggy out of the apartment
(located on Hollywood Blvd. and Hudson Ave.) and Peggy would come
to our house for warmth and food." When asked for more details, Ruth
said, "Being older, I took a protective stance toward Peggy and she would
tell me about her mother…how her mother would lock her out of the

Blondie Brings Up Baby, with Larry Simms as Alexander "Baby Dumpling" Bumstead. (From the collection of Connie Stratton)

house when she was with a friend or drinking. Her mother knew where to find her later in the evening and would come to our house, often in a fury." Ruth added, "I do have a painful memory of her mother... She (more than once) told Peggy, who then told me, that she didn't want her to play with Jews. Not surprisingly, there was a lot of anti-Semitism in Los Angeles at the time."

That same year, Peggy was cast in another small part in the Columbia film *Blondie Brings up Baby*. These may have been bit parts, but each job gave Peggy a little more experience, more exposure, and more credibility.

For nine months of the year, strict child-labor laws required little Peggy to have at least three hours of schooling each day, to be finished by 4:00 p.m. There must be an hour for lunch and an hour for play. A child's workday was over at 5:30 p.m. While she was under contract with a studio, they provided the schooling. Any other time, she attended public school.

Being cast in two films in such rapid succession gave Virginia reason to believe that Peggy was now an established Hollywood actress. She soon learned that that wasn't the case. It took a whole year to get another role.

In the meantime, Virginia was arrested again on April 8, 1939—this time in Beverly Hills for passing six bad checks. She was given six months in the county jail, ordered to pay $386.10 restitution, and would be on probation for five years. Peggy was again placed in the custody of her maternal grandmother. Virginia's jail time was shortened on June 2 by a modification of the terms, and she was released on the condition that she would return to Washington, D.C.

Peggy was given a small part in RKO's *Abe Lincoln in Illinois*, however, so the pair stayed in California.

The Court found out that Virginia was violating the terms of the parole and a Bench Warrant was issued on September 26. Peggy was soon finished with her work on the film, and Virginia then took her and went back east. The warrant was withdrawn on October 17. The film would be released in 1940.

Then the movie offers stopped coming.

The purpose for Virginia being in San Francisco en route to Los Angeles on March 6, 1940, is unknown, but that's the day the police arrested her there for two counts of forgery and violation of probation. She pled guilty to one count and the other was dismissed. Her probation was revoked on June 25 and she was sentenced to one year in the county jail for both counts to run consecutively. On the forgery charge, she was given ten years probation and one year in the county jail, to also run consecutively. The order was modified and Virginia was released from custody on June 10, 1941. It is unclear where Peggy had been staying during all this time, but she was not told that her mother was in jail. All they told her was that she was "away."

They heard nothing from Hollywood for two years, then another small part was offered to Peggy in the Universal production, *Eagle Squadron*. Virginia, now reunited with her daughter, readily accepted. Peggy's part in this one took only one day to film and she was paid twenty-five dollars. This was soon followed by a more substantial role in *The Pied Piper*. Her part was supposed to have gone to another little actress, but that child had come down with the measles so Peggy got the role instead. This was the big career break for Peggy that Virginia had been waiting for. More important, it was on this set that Peggy met a dear, gentle boy who was to become a lifelong friend, Roddy McDowall.

Also on the set was a little Peggy lookalike. She was Peggy's stand-in and Peggy, who loved to give people nicknames, called her "B." B recipro-

So young, but already skillful on ice skates. (From the collection of Mary Eckard)

cated and abbreviated Peggy Ann's name to "Pan." They would work together in two more films after this one, becoming playmates off the set.

Immediately after *The Pied Piper* was done, Virginia felt that now they could finally begin enjoying her daughter's certain future success. The pair moved into the Grand Garden of Allah bungalow hotel, which was well known for housing many of Hollywood's greats, past and present. In that hotel, they had quite an illustrious neighbor, Orson Welles. Welles was working on a screenplay at the time, but seemed completely unimpressed by Peggy, choosing to ignore the little tyke.

On a publicity trip for *The Pied Piper*, Virginia and Peggy stopped in Delaware. Just the place Peggy wanted to be! Her father was working there at Ft. Dupont now, and they had a wonderful reunion. Newsreel footage shows her joyously running into her daddy's outstretched arms.

Ruth Bricker recalls a cute bit of mischief she and Peggy got into once Virginia and Peggy had returned to California: "I had two older sisters (thirteen and fourteen years older) who smoked and dated, and Drucilla, Peggy and I wanted to be teenagers and grow up fast. We took a pack of my sister's cigarettes and Peggy took some liquor from her mom's supply and we walked into the lobby of a nearby elegant hotel, led by Drucilla with glasses in hand, sat in the lobby couches, and lit up and pretended to drink the awful-tasting

A joyous visit with Daddy at Ft. Dix. (From the collection of Mary Eckard)

Having chow with the soldiers at Ft. Dix. (From the collection of Mary Eckard)

stuff. It wasn't long before we were escorted home (they knew my mother) and roundly scolded and warned about how they would let it go this time…but next time the police would take us home. We were scared, but did notice how the family tried hard not to let us see them laughing."

Virginia had high hopes for better and better offers to come Peggy's way when *The Pied Piper* was released in 1942. It didn't happen. Nothing happened. Virginia was running out of money, so now was as good a time as any to go back east. Her probation was modified on July 15, 1942, to permit her to leave California, and they returned to Virginia's parents' house in New York.

CHAPTER 3

In 1943, Orson Welles and Twentieth Century-Fox summoned them to return to Hollywood. They wanted Peggy to test for a part in the film *Jane Eyre*. It seems Welles had watched Peggy more closely than they thought because he now felt that she would be perfect as the young Jane. Virginia borrowed the money to take her daughter back to the west coast. Peggy tested and got the part of Jane Eyre as a child, along with a term contract with Twentieth Century-Fox. Virginia told her that, if she did a good job in this film, she would buy her a typewriter, something Peggy was wishing for.

Of course, Virginia's returning with Peggy to California meant she was violating the terms of her parole, and she was once again arrested. On September 14, 1943, her probation was modified and she began serving a year in the county jail.

Meanwhile, on the set, Peggy was glad to see that her stand-in was again B. There was a wistfulness in Peggy's demeanor now. "I remember her saying when she returned [from the east]," says B, "that she wished they had stayed." It's easy to see why: If they had, her mother would still be free and Peggy would at least be on the same coast as her father. She could very easily have been feeling abandoned by her parents and lonely at this point, even though the studio had provided caregivers for her.

Also appearing in this film was Margaret O'Brien, portraying Adele Varens, the child who was under the care of the adult Jane Eyre. Says she, "I first met Peggy Ann on the set of *Jane Eyre*. Even though we had no scenes together, we had to be there at the same time for a day of wardrobe tests, publicity stills and interviews about the film. Peggy was a very sweet

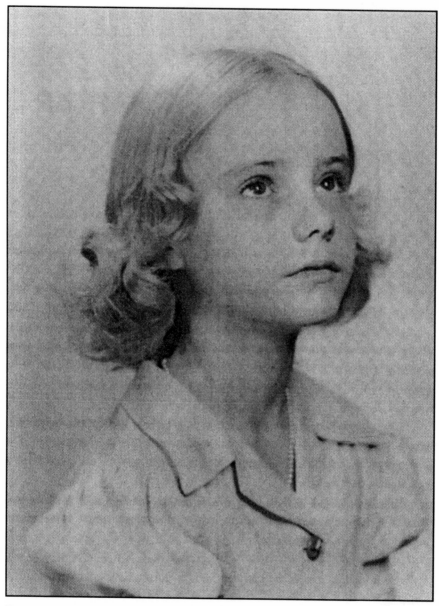

Peggy was very pretty in her own unique way. (From the collection of Connie Stratton)

person, even as a child. She had a gentle side to her personality that remained with her throughout her life. She was essentially kind and sweet every time I was in her company."

In this film, Peggy's ability to cry on cue was of utmost importance. How did she do it, wondered reporters. "I think what will happen to me if I *don't* cry," she replied. In reality, she had plenty to cry about. All she had to do was think of her own precarious situation with her parents.

"Peggy was a dear, modest child," co-star Joan Fontaine writes. "Very quiet, professional and well behaved."

In the film, Peggy appeared in scenes with the beautiful young Elizabeth Taylor. As usual, Peggy was made up to look very plain but, nevertheless, was an exquisite little creature and gave a magnificent performance. Unfortunately, however, an Associated Press article couldn't have done her ego much good. It said "She is plain. Her hair is blonde, but not golden, and it is so honestly straight that any 'normal' movie mamma would rush her to a beauty parlor. Her hazel eyes have no frame of long curly lashes, her nose is too large in her childish face, her eyebrows are uneven and unplucked."

Even though she was a disciplined little actress, she was still a child. "Something wonderful that Peggy and I used to love to do when we were on the set of *Jane Eyre*," says Margaret O'Brien, "was to sneak over to the set of *Song of Bernadette* at Fox. I think they had completed filming at that time but the set remained intact, and Peggy and I loved to play there. It was especially fun for both of us."

When Peggy went home after work, she would sometimes play with her friend Myrna Bowers. The two little girls loved to play dress-up together in their mothers' clothes and pretend to be going to the Mocambo nightclub.

One thing that Margaret noticed early on was Peggy's lack of parental guidance. "I don't ever remember her mother being present," she says, "either at the studio or any of the events we attended. I don't know if this was a bad thing. She always seemed to be okay with the studio people who accompanied her."

Virginia was released from jail early on March 3, 1944, in time for the premiere of *Jane Eyre*. She and Peggy now lived on Spaulding Drive in Beverly Hills, and Peggy had her own portable typewriter; her mother had fulfilled her promise.

In a March 12 article about child stars, the *Akron Beacon Journal* tells its readers about Peggy's new film. "Peggy Ann is worth special attention," theater editor Betty French wrote, "because she is from Canton, is the niece of Mr. and Mrs. Russell Eckard...and also because she looks like the finest juvenile actress to come to the screen in years.

Jane Eyre, with Elizabeth Taylor.

"She plays the role of the young Jane with extreme poignancy, skillfully projecting her shyness and misery and establishing the character so well that Joan Fontaine has little to do in the grown-up sequences.

"Peggy Ann is 12 years old and has outgrown the childish appeal of young Miss O'Brien, and therefore it is genuine ability alone which has won her one fine role after another during the last year."

Some reviewers, in fact, said that Peggy even looked like Joan Fontaine. Did she really, she wondered? She asked people if that meant she would grow up to be pretty like her co-star.

It was in this decade that Peggy was doing her best work. She had matured in the business and understood it much better. Acting, she discovered, was bunches of fun. She was a bright child who learned quickly and always knew her lines perfectly.

Studio head Darryl F. Zanuck dismissed any suggestions that Peggy be given acting lessons. Her naturalness, he felt, was her greatest asset, and dramatic training could destroy that.

So lauded was Peggy's work in this film that MGM wanted to purchase half of her contract from Twentieth Century-Fox so she could star in their upcoming project, *National Velvet*. She and her mother wanted that role so badly they could taste it. It was not to be, however. Zanuck wouldn't allow the contract to be half-sold, so Elizabeth Taylor was cast in

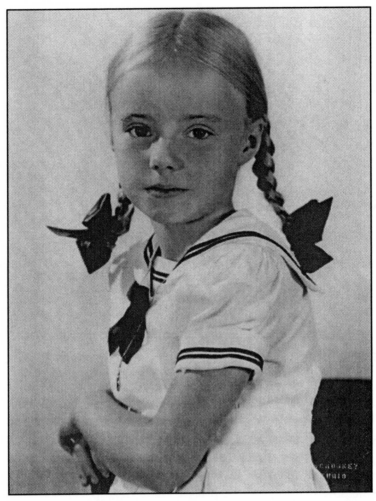

One good thing she could do with straight hair is braid it. (From the collection of Connie Stratton)

the part instead. Irate, Virginia demanded to know why. Because, he explained, they have big plans for Peggy. She would get a bigger and better role than that, he promised.

Before that would happen though, Peggy was cast in *Keys of the Kingdom*, which was also released in 1944. She was happy to learn that Roddy McDowall was in the cast, too.

Gregory Peck worked with them in this motion picture and shared his memories of Peggy: "Her behavior on the set was impeccable. I have the impression of a charming and extremely talented little girl." While some other child stars were known for being obnoxious on the set, little Peggy was every

Margaret O'Brien's *Command Performance* with Frank Sinatra, Elizabeth Taylor
and Peggy. (From the collection of Margaret O'Brien)

bit the professional. Her mother had trained her well. Too, there was no reason to misbehave. Peggy loved it on the set. The cast and crew were like a
family and the set was like a nice, safe home to her. She was treated very well
there. Life at work was much more predictable than life at home was.

On July 16, 1944, Virginia had again caught for passing bad checks—
this time three fictitious ones in Beverly Hills, totaling $343.68. She prom-
ised the judge she would pay restitution if they would let her go. He
agreed and no action was taken.

Back at the studio, Peggy was busy concentrating on her work. It
was usually her mother, however, who would dominate media interviews.
Reporter Dora Albert was assigned to do an article about young Peggy
but, she says, "her mother took command and answered all my questions—while Peggy, a shy twelve-year-old, sat quietly, saying scarcely a
word." When a reporter would ask about her daddy, however, Peggy would
eagerly fetch her wallet and show her Lt. Garner's picture. How she wished
they could be like a real family again.

Virginia liked to tell reporters that she had come from "an Ohio steel
family," but the apparent intended meaning of this—that she was an heir-

ess of some prominence back home—was a bit misleading. What was the family's connection to the steel industry, then? "Our grandfather [Virginia's father] worked in the steel mill as a roller," replied Connie Stratton, the daughter of Virginia's sister.

Virginia and Peggy no longer lived on Spaulding Drive and Virginia was having a difficult time finding another house due to the housing shortage in Hollywood, so they were staying at an auto court. Virginia was working at night, at an undisclosed job, in order to help pay the bills. She was determined to keep Peggy innocent and untouched by Hollywood, but Virginia herself would do whatever was necessary to promote her daughter's career and to put food on the table. Peggy had a difficult time sleeping at night during that time, worrying about where her mother was. When Zanuck found out about their situation, they were immediately given the little four-room bungalow which Shirley Temple had once used. It was right across the street from the studio. Peggy loved it! To a child, this was a dream house. It was scaled to child proportions with two bedrooms and a huge living room with a pink fireplace, and in the backyard was a swing. Since there was no rent to pay, working was now unnecessary for Virginia. Cleaning, gardening and laundry services were provided; all Virginia had to do was make breakfast and help Peggy learn her lines. They had lunch at the studio commissary and dinner at a Beverly Hills restaurant.

This little house had another tenant, too—a cat named Mr. Whiskers. They also had a dog named Wags, but his stay was cut short due to his bad habit of digging under the picket fence, getting out, and chasing the studio cat. This cat, says a press release, had influential friends; so off to the kennel went Wags. He was soon replaced by a dog they named Mutt.

A cheery press release quotes Peggy as saying, "There isn't another girl in the world who has a yard of 300 acres, with miles of streets, projection rooms where they'll let you slip in now and then and see a movie no one but the studio people have seen. And dozens of policemen patrolling the 'estate' at night, and famous stars walking past your front yard every day!" Sundays was another story, though. The place felt deserted then.

An avid fan of juvenile mystery stories, Peggy could read one in two and a half hours flat. Put her together with a piano and she could play boogie-woogie tunes by ear. She also enjoyed sports—tennis, horseback riding, swimming, and especially skating. She was a very accomplished ice skater, having won a medal at a Westwood skating meet. In addition, she collected stamps, perfume bottles, and books by Noel Coward. That wasn't all, either. She was also very much into ballet, with no less than the famous Russian choreographer Adolf Bohm as her teacher, according to a press release. The same press release said that Olympic champion Vivi-Anne Hulten was Peggy's ice skating instructor. Truth or hype?

Peggy's stay in this house was to end when the filming of this picture did, so Virginia again went house-hunting. Her daughter was earning $1,000 per week now, so she could surely afford a nice house, Virginia thought. Soon she found exactly what she wanted.

In compliance with the Coogan Law, the court was in control of Peggy's money, and she would have to get their permission to buy this house. Virginia took Peggy with her to court to ask that the $40,000 she would earn under her forty-week contract this year be used to buy a house in Brentwood. It was a beautiful house; she just had to have it, Virginia said. The judge, Henry M. Willis, responded "I cannot approve a situation in which the child's earnings will be frozen into $40,000 worth of unproductive real estate. I think that at least 25% of her income should go into a trust. After all, the contract only runs for a year. The studio may never exercise its option. The income may stop. If it's a trust, it stays there." Virginia pleaded with him, but he stood firm. "This house would be just a showplace and not for her. She would have no use for it until she is much older. In a house like this your scale of living would have to go up." Virginia asked also for $6,500 from Peggy's bank account to furnish the house. This was denied. The judge told her to find a less-costly house of around $18,000.

"But who wants to live in a $18,000 house?" Virginia sniffed indignantly. She felt that such paltry accommodations weren't worthy of Peggy Ann Garner, the movie star. The duo left with Virginia's dreams of splendor thwarted.

True to their word, Twentieth Century-Fox executives soon cast Peggy in a film called *A Tree Grows in Brooklyn*. Virginia told her that, if she did a good job in this film, she would buy Peggy her own pair of professional ice skates. It was that, not the paycheck, that would motivate the child.

This is the film that would change Peggy's life.

CHAPTER 4

According to a feature article about Peggy in the October 1944 issue of *Screenland*, *A Tree Grows in Brooklyn*'s Francie was "the most important role ever written for a juvenile player." It was to be Elia Kazan's first directing job in Hollywood, and the result would later be deemed one of the best, most successful films of the decade. It would, in fact, become a classic that no remake has ever equaled.

Kazan was very fond of Peggy, as was everyone else on the set. In an interview about this film years later, he told reporter Jeff Young that Peggy's face was the most authentic thing about *A Tree Grows in Brooklyn*; she was the best part of the film. Thomas G. Aylesworth seems to agree in his book *Hollywood's Kids*. He said that, even though there were major adult stars in the film, it was Peggy's presence that dominated it.

Peggy had a remarkable and unusual talent that was noted by *Screenland*'s reporter, Mollie Merrick: She had the uncanny ability to make herself look like whoever was playing her onscreen mother. This is especially noticeable in the film *In Name Only*, in which her mother was played by Carole Lombard. It was the mannerisms, Peggy told her. If she takes on the woman's speech patterns and move in the same manner as her screen mother, she will *seem* to look like her.

In this October 1944, *Screenland* article entitled "Awkward Age Star," Merrick describes how Peggy did this for her role as Francie:

> [Peggy said] "You see if people do the same little things in the same way, people are going to think they look alike even if they really don't. They are alike, and that's the important thing.

Dorothy McGuire has a way with her eyes. And she often leaves the ends of her sentences trailing in the air..."

And as she talked, Peggy Ann Garner became Dorothy McGuire's daughter. It is not mimicry alone. It's a trick of projecting her personality into the personality of the individual she has in mind. It is the secret of her amazing performances in previous pictures—performances that have brought her the fattest plum Hollywood has to give in 1944. *Francie*, born in bitter poverty on dingy Brooklyn alleys, fights the neighborhood kids like a wild-cat for a place at the stale bread counter, gathers junk which she sells the local dealer, bargaining shrewdly for the odd half-cent. *Francie*, torn by dreams, finds beauty in the persistent leafing of a green tree in the grimy expanse of brick and concrete that is her world. *Francie's* heart is heavy because her father comes home "sick" so often and the other children on the block jeer and taunt her about it. *Francie* is a product of the slum, wise and sad and grave and gay—knowing stern facts before she should, disposing of them in the child trick of make-believe. It's a role for any actress to envy—a role which can carry her straight on up into twinkling lights on the marquees and a salary bracket less easily budgeted than her present one.

The title of this article told a story, too. Peggy was at the age at which most child stars disappear from the screen—the awkward early-adolescent years. While Peggy did, of course, experience a metamorphosis from child to woman, it was a gentle transition. Not only was she able to continue acting throughout her teen years, but that was when she did her best work.

In *The New York Times*, Bosley Crowther wrote: "Through a truly surpassing little actress, Peggy Ann Garner, on whom the camera mostly stays, the producers have ably provided a sensitive mirror for the reflection of childish moods and for all the personal comprehension of the pathos of poverty. Little Miss Garner, with her plain face and lank hair, is Miss Smith's Francie Nolan to the life." It was Peggy's naturalness that made her so appealing and so right for this role.

Kazan made it a point to get to know the actors, but in a casual, nonthreatening way. Before long, they would open up to him, giving him the insight into their inner workings that he needed to know in order to

A Tree Grows in Brooklyn, with Dorothy McGuire and Ted Donaldson

coax the best performance out of them. During the session he had with Peggy, he learned that she yearned very much to have her father near. The war was going on and he was in the military, so she worried constantly about his well-being. When the scene called for Peggy to cry, Kazan used this knowledge and devised the perfect motivation for her—without actually saying so, he planted the idea in her mind that her father might be killed in the line of duty. It produced the desired results. In fact, it worked *too* well. Peggy was crying so hard in the graduation scene that she couldn't stop after Kazan called "Cut!" Kindhearted co-star Joan Blondell had to comfort her for ten minutes before the tears stopped.

Kazan didn't need to motivate James Dunn, who played Peggy's father. Dunn loved Peggy as he would his own child, and those feelings shown through in his character. As Crowther's review continued, "In the radiant performance of these two actors of a dreamy adoration between father and child is achieved a pictorial demonstration of emotion that is sublimely eloquent."

Almost thirteen now, Peggy was outgrowing her pale blonde hair and blue eyes. She now had light ash-brown hair and grey-green eyes,

The affection between Peggy and James Dunn, her screen dad, was real.

which fit the part of Francie in this picture quite well. Peggy had to carry it solely on her talent and personality as she was purposely made to look as plain as possible in it. No problem. She handled it like a seasoned pro. As usual, she learned her lines quickly and well.

B was Peggy's stand-in in this film, as she had been in two previous pictures. Because B was from a family that was quite respected in Hollywood, Virginia allowed Peggy to go over to their house to play. Once Virginia had seen Peggy safely to B's home and left, the girls would have a wonderful time doing the things that regular, everyday kids did but that Peggy wasn't allowed to do. They would often go over to the nearby vacant lot and climb trees and play Kick the Can. The two were also known to sneak over to the Hitching Post cinema a time or two, too. "She was a different person than on the set," B says. "Peggy flew, she just flew. I flew with her." She added, "Peggy put on a mask [on the set], I feel. I think she was herself when we got together."

There is a lot of downtime when one is working on a film. Lights must be adjusted, discussions are held, and various other things get in the way of actual acting time. Peggy and B found a way to pass that time. They learned to knit and were practicing their new skill by jointly making a scarf. While B was standing in place for the adjustments to the set, Peggy would be sitting off to the side, knitting away. Once Peggy was called to the set, B took up where Peggy left off. "I ended up as the owner of our scarf," B says. "It went on and on for about twenty-two feet before we thought our knitting was professional enough to attempt other things."

Even though Peggy and B had great times together, B says, "Peggy had a lot of sadness about her, even when she was young." Because she missed her father, perhaps? B responded, "She talked to me quite a bit about it. I had lost my father to an automobile accident when I was young, and even though Peggy's father was alive, she felt this sadness. Yes, it was a tragedy in Peggy's life, I believe, to be taken away [from him] like that."

Once Virginia found out that the girls were climbing trees, she hit the roof. "She went crazy," B says. "Told her how valuable her 'limbs' were and if she had scratched herself, a whole week of shooting would be lost." No more was Peggy allowed to visit B's home. "After that, I was picked up in a car to go with Peggy to such places as Griffith Park, where there were always photographers to take the inevitable, unposed photos of a child enjoying free time. I was told by her mother to keep my back to the camera."

B continues, "If we went shopping and Peggy bought something, she always insisted that I have the same thing. I had a favorite bathing suit, one of her gifts, for years."

The girls also went to the Polar Palace on weekends to do some ice skating. B was quite impressed with Peggy's skating skill.

While Peggy and her screen brother, Ted Donaldson, were having lunch at the commissary one day, a handsome young soldier in uniform entered the room and was warmly greeted as he went from table to table to visit with his old friends. There was a *Movie Stars Parade* magazine photographer in attendance, recording the event. This twenty-one-year-old man was Lon McCallister, who had been an actor for eight years but was now serving in the military. He and some of his fellow GIs were in town to make a film called *Winged Victory*. Pigtailed Peggy didn't know it at the time, but Lon would later become a very dear friend of hers, too.

In the seventy-three-day shooting schedule for *A Tree Grows in Brook-lyn*, Peggy was involved in seventy-one of them, which made this the longest child's role in movie history to that time. So exemplary was her work in this film that critics from coast-to-coast would lavish praise on Peggy for her intuitive, sensitive, mature performance. "*Tree* was very trying and it took a long time to complete," B recalls. "Peggy was a real pro and I think, for once, Peggy's mother saw the strain this had on her daughter. She was quite kind to Peggy and praised her. I had never heard her do this before. The only words I heard from her before were critical."

Of Peggy's work in this exceptional motion picture, actor/producer Jeff Howard says, "Every time I watch that film I think of something that my favorite acting teacher used to drill into us all the time. She always said that it isn't the 'big picture' or the total performance that endears a character to an audience—it is the small moments, little nuances that come out to define the character. 'To hell with the big picture! Find the moments, find the moments!' she would yell at us. She was so right. And it takes constant work and intense concentration. Peggy had it licked. As Francie she finds moment, after moment, after moment…tiny subtleties whether it be a look, a line delivery or a minute action that totally endears that character to an audience. Her performance is an essay in 'finding the moment.'"

Howard cites an example: "Most striking about her performance in *A Tree Grows in Brooklyn* is the non-verbal acting Peggy Ann does. There are brilliant moments of this throughout the film but the scene that comes to mind at this moment is when Francie is on her way out of the apartment on the night of her father's death and her mother stops her and tries to reassure her, telling her that 'I'll have to be mama and papa to you now.' That slow turn, and that cold stare that hurls icy daggers, causes her mother to shrink back and avert her eyes. A powerful, powerful scene."

Professional reviewers agreed. *Variety* wrote: "There have been few pictures to tug at the heartstrings as this one does," pointing out that "Upon Francie, Miss Smith has lavished much of the story's sympathies, and the young actress performs capitally."

This would be the last picture in which B and Peggy would work together. B's mother, a career woman, was moving east and B would go with her. Peggy gifted her pal with a very ornate golden charm bracelet, on which were charms that had special meanings to them. The bus charm, for instance, represented the method of transportation used for the film's crew members when taken to on-location work, the cowboy and Indian headdress charms would forever remind B of their clandestine trips to the Hitching Post Theater, and a heart charm was engraved with the initials B and P. "Peggy was a good friend. She was a very sweet person, very thoughtful person," says B.

The cast later repeated *A Tree Grows in Brooklyn* for CBS radio on a show called *Hollywood Star Time*.

CHAPTER 5

Twentieth Century increased Peggy's weekly salary to $1,250 for the next six months. Her take-home pay was not as high as most people would think, however. It was only 50 percent of the gross. Ten percent went to her agent, 20 percent to withholding tax, and 20 percent to victory bonds. The balance went into her trust fund (per her father's request), from which her mother was given $500 each month to spend on Peggy. Whenever the child wanted money for something, she would ask Virginia for it. Peggy's requests were usually quite modest—with one exception.

For Christmas, Peggy didn't want the usual things girls her age did. Instead, she wanted an emerald. No, thought Virginia, that wouldn't be appropriate for such a young girl. Instead, she got her a cats-eye ring.

A gala party was thrown on Peggy's thirteenth birthday, and both parents were in attendance. The media was there as well, snapping photos of the trio that would grace a feature article months later in *Photoplay's* July 1945 issue.

In a picture of Peggy kissing her uniformed dad, it was evident that he was now a Lieutenant in the U.S. Army Military Police. Lieutenant Garner had recently been transferred to the West Coast, so was able to see his daughter more often. His job was to act as counsel for the government as plaintiff against those who had military-discipline charges. Whatever the reason, Peggy was still very, very happy to have her father back.

On February 26, 1945, Peggy was featured, along with Elizabeth Taylor and Margaret O'Brien, in a *Life* magazine article entitled "Three

Little Movie Girls." She was hailed as the most perfect example of the film industry's turning away from adorable children to more realistic ones. Her mouth was a bit too wide, they said, she had a ski-jump nose and her hair was straight. She was just the kind of actress with whom young moviegoers could identify. The photo spread illustrated Peggy's hobbies and interests—bicycling, skating, swimming, and doll collecting. (This was a bit misleading, however. She didn't own a bike and, according to a friend, Peggy was posing with dolls that were not hers.) Her allowance, the magazine reported, was $1.50 per week and she usually spent it on mystery books. She had an active mind and liked to exercise it.

Before bed each night, Peggy would write about her day in her journal, then it was lights out at 9:00.

There were at least two big premieres for *A Tree Grows in Brooklyn*—one at Grauman's Chinese Theater in Hollywood and another in New York City on February 28, 1945. The public instantly fell in love with Peggy. Soon, she was easily recognized and was unable to go around town without causing a stir. Therefore, it was Virginia's policy to bring friends to Peggy, rather than have her go to them.

Always happy to give an autograph to a soldier.

At a big premiere, with Mom behind her [From the collection of Connie Stratton]

Helen W. Pine interviewed the young star for *Movie Show*. Peggy told her, "There was this boy in New York—when I was staying with Mother at the Sherry-Netherlands. He came clear from Brooklyn every day and he lurked, watching what time I went out and what time I came in and everything. He brought me a big box of chocolates one day and another time he brought some roses. I found the nicest picture of myself I possibly could—before he even asked for one—and I autographed it and gave it to him." Peggy appreciated the fact that he just watched her instead of rushing up or tugging at her, like some fans did.

She was also interviewed by *L. A. Times* reporter James F. Denton in April 1945. After the usual questions and answers, Peggy enlisted Denton's help in convincing her mother that she should have a bicycle of her own.

Being interviewed by Mary Margaret McBride.

She had presented plenty of reasons why she needed a bike, but felt that another adult might have more influence on the woman than she did. No luck. "It's too dangerous," was Virginia's final answer.

At this time of life, Peggy was starting to have frequent disagreements with her mother. She had been plain long enough. She wanted to be more like a normal teenaged girl. She wanted to fix her hair nicely and wear dresses that were longer and less little-girlish. She wanted to wear jewelry. Virginia would have none of it. She said that it was Peggy's plainness that had been responsible for her success in movies, so that's the way it was to stay.

"Even after Peggy had achieved fame after *A Tree Grows in Brooklyn*," recalls her friend Ruth Bricker, "her mother kept exploiting her with very little show of love, care or affection."

Perhaps looks didn't matter, when it came to boys—or at least for Danny Shaw, who had a small part in *Tree* and, according to the press, was Peggy's first boyfriend. For the duration of the filming, Peggy had been intentionally kept pale and wan, dressed in cast-off clothing, and had her hair kept straggly. She didn't mind that for the filming, but had been afraid that Danny would think that was her normal look. The studio promised her pretty clothes and curly hair in her next picture, however, so that pacified her.

With George Raft and Joan Bennett in *Nob Hill*.

Once *A Tree Grows in Brooklyn* had wrapped, Peggy had two days to relax, then was back to work. The good job she had done in *Tree* led to a role as an Irish immigrant in the 1945 film, *Nob Hill*. At last she would have curls and pretty clothes! This part required her to have an Irish accent, which she picked up right away and performed beautifully.

Director Henry Hathaway arranged a very special surprise for Peggy. On the day she was to do the scene in which she appears glamorous for the first time on film, bedecked in a beautiful party dress, William Garner was there on the set to cheer her on. That, she felt, was one of her greatest thrills. It was the first time her father had ever seen her before the camera.

Later that year, Peggy was cast in the delightful film *Junior Miss*, which was also a favorite of many of Peggy's fans. The film rights to this hit Broadway play were bought especially for Peggy by Twentieth Century-Fox, and she received top billing for the first time ever. They even wrote in an ice-skating sequence because of her skating expertise.

It was on the set of *Junior Miss* that she met Barbara Whiting for the first time. "I was kind of enamored of meeting her, like any young kid would be," Barbara says. Not only was this their first meeting, but it was

A surprise reunion with her beloved daddy. (From the collection of Connie Stratton)

also Barbara's first film. With a personality very similar to that of her lively "Fuffy" character, she was a natural for the part. The two girls were together both on the set and in the studio's schoolroom, and they hit it off right away, soon becoming close, lifelong friends. Watching Peggy at work was a crash course in acting for Barbara, and the duo exhibited excellent comedic timing.

In this upbeat picture, Peggy's character wore a long, formal dress in the final scene. Once the movie cameras were turned off, she was delighted to pose for dozens of still photos in this dream gown. "Why shouldn't I have the same privilege in real life?" she wondered. Peggy tried to convince her mother of the merits of owning such a gorgeous dress. "You're too young," said Virginia. Nevertheless, Peggy soon had a beauti-

The beautiful *Junior Miss* gown was given to Peggy as a gift.

ful long dress of her own, three years ahead of schedule, thanks to the benevolence of Twentieth Century-Fox, who gave her the white dress she had worn in the film.

She may have been in adolescent films wearing a long dress, but Hollywood didn't want anything to interfere with her wholesome image. On this issue, Virginia agreed. They took pains to keep her as naive and innocent as possible, as they did with all of their child stars. As long as

A dynamic duo indeed! Peggy and pal Barbara Whiting in the hilarious
romp entitled *Junior Miss.*

they maintained their youthful charm, they would continue to be good
moneymakers for the studio.

Peggy was driven to the studio by her mother each morning. While
on the set, she had her own tutor. When filming was in progress, but she
was not needed on the set, she attended the studio schoolroom in the Old
Writers Building. What made this school even better was that Peggy was
very fond of her teacher, Francis Klampt, whose class walls were covered
with photos of the famous children that she had taught. Mrs. Klampt
made history come alive, and it quickly became Peggy's favorite subject.
Math was her least favorite. Nevertheless, Peggy was a very bright child
and a straight-A student. She also went the extra mile by serving as reporter for the school newspaper, *Fox Fun.*

Peggy's favorite part of the workday was lunch at the lively commissary, but the friends she had in her non-working world were rarely actors.
Barbara Whiting and Roddy McDowall were exceptions to that, but Peggy
made it a point not to "talk shop" when her non-acting peers were around
so they wouldn't feel out of place. Throughout her life, Peggy would always
be very sensitive to others' feelings and did her best to do what was right.

Top billing at age thirteen!

Peggy endeared herself to everyone on the set. (From the collection of Mary Eckard)

Once the filming of *Junior Miss* was done, the studio announced that it would do a sequel sometime in the future. "That would have been great to do that character again," said Barbara Whiting to writer Laura Wagner. "After all, I was basically playing myself. Of course, working with Peggy Ann again would have been absolutely fun. We got along so well together." The girls were best friends now. Unfortunately, the sequel never happened.

Sunday, May 20, was a fun day. Peggy and fellow child-star Margaret O'Brien appeared together at the Los Angeles Coliseum for "I Am An American Day." This was an annual event held throughout the country to commemorate the loyalty of Americans to the spirit of justice and equality of their great country.

Peggy continued to make appearances, and received the resulting letter from the Skouras Theatres Corporation in New York City:

June 15, 1945

Miss Peggy Ann Garner
Hotel Sherry Netherland
59th Street & 5th Avenue
New York, N.Y.

Dear Peggy Ann:

Thank you so much for appearing at the Park Plaza and Astoria theatres last Wednesday evening. Everyone was thrilled at your performance. You made our Rallies a huge success and I cannot express enough my deep appreciation to you.

We would very much like to have you and your mother come and spend next Sunday, June 17th, with us in the Country. My brother, Plato, will take you out for a sail and afterwards you can take a nice long swim. We want you both to stay for dinner as well.

Looking forward to seeing you and your mother on Sunday, I am

Sincerely yours,
Caphne Dolores Skouras

Soon afterward, Virginia made news of her own. She announced through Hedda Hopper's column that she was going to have a baby. She had felt ill, she said, so was seen by a doctor who diagnosed pregnancy.

This was apparently an incorrect diagnosis as the baby never materialized.

CHAPTER 6

Peggy was delighted to revisit her old hometown and received a heroine's welcome. The *Canton Repository* ran a feature article about her in its July 3, 1945 issue. Complete with four photos of her in various activities, the article was entitled "Young Star's Visit Opens With a Busy, Happy Day." Although Peggy considered this visit a four-day vacation, it was a working one. She and her mother were officially there for the Canton premiere of *Nob Hill* and they had a very full schedule.

The city rolled out the red carpet for Peggy. Flashbulbs were going off everywhere as she was given a big lunch party and presented with the key to the city, a gold badge making her an honorary member of the police department, and a scroll that named her Canton's #1 citizen. The teen departments of the city's stores proclaimed Peggy Ann Days. They allowed her to use a bicycle, and she gleefully rode it all over town. How she wished she could have a bike of her own! Peggy did a radio interview, then went to the Aultmann Hospital, where she had been born, to see her cousin, nurse Marilyn Muse, and they were photographed together during this joyous reunion.

"Her happiest times were in Canton," Marilyn recalls, "because that's where she could be a child and get away from the Hollywood bit. At our house, she could just relax and enjoy herself." Relaxation would come later. For now, though, her schedule was full and the camera's eye was always on her.

A friend of Bill Garner's gifted Peggy with a pea jacket that, even though it was too large for her, became her very favorite wrap. She would wear it often.

On the final day of this stop was the *Nob Hill* premiere at the Palace Theater. While preparing for it in her flower-filled hotel suite, Peggy was scheduled to be interviewed by the *Akron Beacon Journal* theater editor Betty French. Ms. French walked in early and found Peggy sitting on the sofa with her feet curled under her. "Yipe!" she exclaimed when she noticed the entrance of the reporter. Peggy then scurried into an adjoining room to cover her bobby-pinned hair with a scarf. That done, she returned to the sofa, ready for her interview. She was accompanied by her mother.

"She looked much taller and older than the sweet little Irish girl I had seen on the screen the night before," wrote Ms. French in the resulting article. "And much more frisky and flippant than the soulful little girls she played on the screen. In fact, she acted exactly like any jittery, inquisitive teenager with too much energy and above-average intelligence." When Virginia left the room, Peggy then settled down, becoming calm and quite professional.

In response to questions, she told Ms. French all about her experiences working in pictures. *A Tree Grows in Brooklyn* was a wonderful film, she told her, and there wasn't a temperamental person to be found anywhere on the set. "Wonderful" was how she also described *Tree* director Elia Kazan and *Junior Miss* director George Seaton. They were her very favorite directors.

The interview was then interrupted by people from Twentieth Century-Fox, who came to take Peggy to the pre-premiere dinner. Peggy obligingly went into another room to get dressed. Ms. French described her return: "When she came back she was wearing a grown-up formal, with a stiff white net skirt and a blue satin bodice with a long blue satin sash in back. Her light brown hair was combed out long and fluffy, she had on a little pink lipstick, her clear tanned skin glowed, and she looked like any very pretty teenager. She said her skirt was too stiff, and her mother said it wasn't, and told her to be careful not to sit on her sash."

When the reporter went downstairs with her for the dinner, they were met by Helen, a twelve-year-old Canton friend of Peggy's. How Helen admired Peggy's gorgeous dress! "Thank you very much," Peggy responded. "I don't dare sit on my sash." On the young star's wrist was a gold charm bracelet and on her left finger was a friendship ring. Helen had noticed that, so chances are that Virginia would, too. Peggy consequently decided to take the ring off before her mother saw it. Helen commented sadly that she didn't have any friendship rings. That tugged at Peggy's heart. "You want to go friendship with me?" Peggy asked. "You know—you give me a ring and I give you one and we go friendship." Before Helen could respond, however, Virginia came over and quietly reminded her daughter of the four people she was to thank at the dinner and what she was to say about them. Then they proceeded to the event as Peggy was softly repeating her mother's instructions to herself, setting them firmly in her mind.

They would return soon for a real vacation but, in the meantime, Peggy was scheduled to promote *Nob Hill* and *Junior Miss* elsewhere. Quoting the July 21, 1945 issue of *New Dynamo* magazine:

"Few new stars have been busier than Peggy Ann Garner was in the 29 days she spent in New York, meeting newspaper folks, posing for pictorial stories for *Life* (this week's issue) at Coney Island, for an exploratory tour of New York City for *Look* Magazine (September issue), the cover of Miss America's fashion layout for *Harper's Bazaar*, etc., etc. She was the guest of honor at 17 luncheons and dinners sponsored by various organizations and for the press not only in New York, but also in Pittsburgh, Harrisburg (Pa.), and other cities where she made personal appearances at bond rallies and in connection with showing of *Nob Hill*.

"She met several hundred exhibitors and many more movie editors, reporters, publishers, etc. She 'threw' a party for the children of editors and publishers of magazines and newspapers in New York, at which *Junior Miss* was shown. She was guest-star on 47 radio broadcasts, 11 of them Coast-to-Coast; she gave interviews to scores of writers in New York and other cities she visited. She shook hands with governors and mayors, was proclaimed Canton's No. 1 citizen by the head of that municipality."

It was exhausting!

There was one more commitment: On August 1, she, Lloyd Nolan (fellow *Tree* player), Carole Landis, Faye Marlowe (from *Junior Miss*), Dick Haymes and other stars and state politicians would join Governor Lausche in Columbus for the world premiere of *Captain Eddie* (in which Nolan was featured).

Once done with all that, they could now go back to Canton for a much-needed three-week furlough.

"Her activities are almost innumerable," wrote reporter Dennis R. Smith, who tried his best to keep up with Peggy. "She rides [a horse] like a veteran and Mr. Bolender was enthusiastic in his praise of the way she

Peggy was welcomed with much fanfare. (From the collection of Connie Stratton)

put one of his best show horses through its paces although most of her previous riding had been done on western cow ponies. Her bicycling, as might be expected, is expert enough to cut corners and do feats that make spectators a little uneasy. She handles a boat as though she were brought up on water; she is an expert skater either on ice or rollers; she plays hot boogie-woogie on the piano, she sings with a really charming voice and she does impersonations that are irresistible."

Once the reporters were gone, Virginia and Peggy enjoyed visiting with their relatives again. It was good to see the Muses, who were the children and grandchildren of Grandma Craig's brother. Peggy had especially looked forward to seeing her Aunt Catherine Eckard, her father's sister, who was a registered nurse at Aultmann Hospital.

Catherine was very British. "A true lady," says her daughter-in-law, Mary Eckard. "She almost always wore a dress." Catherine's only child was a son named David, who was nine years younger than Peggy. "He was just a cute kid and Peggy Ann loved him dearly," says Mary. "She used to love to come there [to Portage Lake, near Akron]. She and David would swim and play in the yard when she was a child."

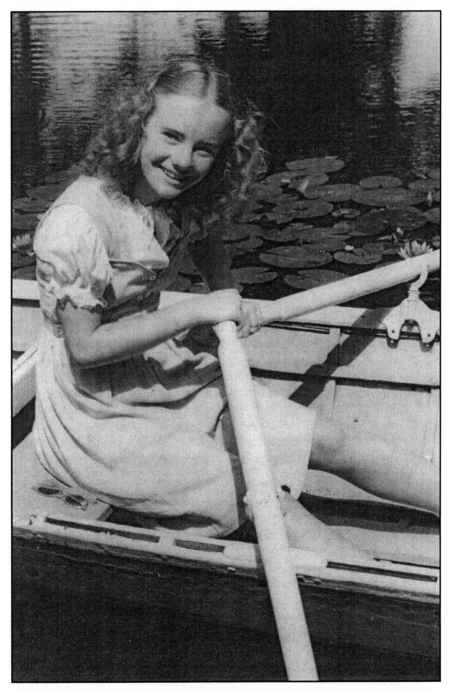

Peggy loved outdoor activities. (From the collection of Connie Stratton)

Time out for a family reunion. Front: Cameron Brogden Jr, Richard Craig, Joy
Craig, and Connie Brogden. Middle: Bertha Muse, Grandpa Craig, Virginia Garner,
Grandma Garner, Peggy, and Grandma Craig. Back: Betty Muse, Helen Brogden,
Sota Muse, Margaret Craig, Karl Craig, Floyd Muse, and Cameron Muse.
(From the collection of Connie Stratton)

With her favorite aunt, Catherine Eckard. (From the collection of Mary Eckard)

In viewing the Garner family's home movies of this era, you could confidently bet that, whenever there was a dog in the picture, Peggy would be nearby. She had so much love to give and pets were often the lucky recipients of her affections. The dogs' excitedly wagging tails indicated that her affection was gladly reciprocated.

"She was fun to be around," says her cousin, Betty Muse Eschliman. "Peggy and Virginia would stay at my family's house. We had a pond, and Peggy loved to go out on it."

And, of course, Peggy and Virginia would spend time with Virginia's sister, Helen. Assuming that her sister would want to help her out however she could, Virginia went shopping and bought three $100 blouses and several other items, charging them to Helen's account. Unfortunately,

Peggy just adored her little cousin David, who was Aunt Catherine's son.
(From the collection of Mary Eckard)

Peggy had lots of love to give to her pets. (From the collection of Mary Eckard)

The Garner family's lake home. (From the collection of Mary Eckard)

Teaching her cousins how to fish. (From the collection of Mary Eckard)

this was done without Helen's permission or knowledge. She found out about it after the fact, when a department store employee called about the strange transaction.

Peggy was flying high. The prestigious *Life* magazine ran a nice photo spread near the center of the magazine, and a picture of Peggy, contentedly riding a merry-go-round, graced the cover of their July 23, 1945 issue. *Junior Miss* was also featured as a picture-story in that issue. Peggy would also appear on the cover of the *Miss America* magazine's November issue.

Box office receipts for *Junior Miss* were fantastic. During its pre-release at the Rivoli Theatre in New York, it was a smash hit. The promotions the studio was doing, plus word-of-mouth advertising, were paying

off as ticket sales in the fourth week surpassed the first week's by $2,111. Even though the rain outside was relentless during the fifth week, the film was still doing well. The team of Peggy Ann Garner and Barbara Whiting could not be beat.

While, earlier, Peggy had been runner-up in the Best Actress category from the New York Film Critics for her work in *A Tree Grows in Brooklyn*, she was now a full-fledged winner. She was awarded the *Film Daily*'s Critics Award for her performances in *Jane Eyre, A Tree Grows in Brooklyn,* and *Junior Miss*. Peggy had repeatedly delivered superior performances.

Virginia took great enjoyment basking in the reflected glory of Peggy's success. All of her hard work was at last paying off, and she could now feel that she was "somebody."

Virginia saw it as *their* career, not just Peggy's. During media interviews, she would often answer the questions while her daughter sat mutely by. The two lived at 229 S. Canon Drive in Beverly Hills, and Peggy was receiving about 1,300 pieces of fan mail each week. Her income ranged from $15,000 to $50,000 per year, and she was being represented by the Feldman-Blum Agency. Virginia engaged the services of a designer to make Peggy's clothes. When they were outgrown, Virginia would send them to her sister's daughter, Connie.

Even the races at Hollywood Park were honoring Peggy. Their sixth race on the afternoon of October 13 was to be named after Peggy Ann Garner. In the lineup for this competition were the horses Capt. Absolute, Reward Me, War Valor, Fuego, Mason Dixon, Autocrat, Sammy Angott, Shut Up, Florizan Beau, and Miracle Kin.

The October 16, 1945 issue of *Look* carried a three-page, many-pictured article about Peggy. While she had been on the studio-related visit to New York that summer, the *Look* photographer had followed her throughout the day and recorded on film her many activities. The spread showed Peggy having breakfast at the Automat, trying out a beautiful long dress at Saks Fifth Avenue, visiting the New Yorker Hotel (where her mother had worked a decade earlier), checking out records at Schirmer's and animals at the Central Park Zoo, then having dinner at the Astor Roof. When she was taken to Brooklyn, she marveled at how similar the real streets of Brooklyn were to the set of *A Tree Grows in Brooklyn*. The set designers had certainly known what they were doing! So normal was Peggy, said the magazine, that she bit her fingernails, collected records, and swooned over Peter Lawford, just like most girls her age.

In fact, Peggy and Barbara Whiting had been hanging out with some friends at an ice cream parlor once when it became known that Lawford had gone into Le Rue's right next door. Of course the two girls went out front to watch him when he came out. "What a dreamboat!" they sighed from a distance as he left the establishment.

Peggy's efforts to promote the sale of war bonds had not gone unappreciated. She received a certificate from the United States Treasury Department that read "For patriotic cooperation rendered in behalf of the War Finance Program this citation is awarded to Peggy Ann Garner. Given under my hand and seal on November 10, 1945." It was signed by the Secretary of the Treasury and the State Chairman.

On January 30, 1946, *Look* magazine threw a party for Peggy and Barbara. Peggy's singing idol Dick Haymes presented her with her first orchid for the occasion, with an attached note that said "Love, Dick Haymes." A few days later, on February 5, the *Look* Achievement Awards for 1945 were presented at the Cathay Circle Theatre. Host Bob Hope presented awards to Ingrid Bergman (actress), Ray Milland (actor), Billy Wilder (director), Joseph Pasternak (producer), Louis B. Mayer (industry), Barbara Hale (newcomer), John Seitz (cinematographer), and Peggy Ann Garner (child actress). In her scrapbook, along with the program that listed the individuals honored, Peggy added this note, "I got a beautiful gold plaque."

The February issue of *Miss America* magazine carried a nice article about Peggy. Fourteen-year-old Sandra Marks had interviewed her as a peer, rather than the usual adult journalist. There were giggles and girl-talk abundant. The resulting title of the piece was "Girl Meets Girl." Peggy confided to Sandra that Dick Haymes was "my present dream boy" and she usually spent her five-dollar allowance on records, Victory stamps, and little gifts for her mother. She showed her silver charm bracelet to Sandra, who counted more than sixty charms on it. "Making cookies is a pet hobby and no amount of failure can discourage her," wrote the cub reporter. "Peggy said her cookies are probably the reason for the number of illnesses at 20th Century-Fox but we'll keep our own ideas on that." A fun interview it was!

Then Peggy and five other juvenile stars, including Barbara, were interviewed for an article in the March 1946 issue of *Miss America*. The topic was "When I Grow Up":

"Oh, there are so many wonderful things about being grown up," Peggy Ann began enthusiastically, "that I don't know where to begin. I want to wear high heels and sophisticated clothes and have my hair on top

Peggy joined the milkman in selling Victory Bonds.
(From the collection of Mary Eckard)

of my head. I want to go around the world and visit all of the out-of-the-way spots. I want to win a cup for ice skating. And I want to go on acting. If I happen to turn out to be attractive when I'm older and am still an actress, that'll be swell. And I wouldn't mind playing character parts when I am so old I have wrinkles."

Peggy Ann paused for a moment and then said, "I must confess that being grown up means that I'll have no more homework to do. But, to prove that I'm sort of a contradictory person, I want to go to college. That is something I insist upon doing even if I continue to work in pictures. An education is awfully important."

It was plain to see what a good team Peggy and Barbara were, and they were soon cast together in another film—*Home, Sweet Homicide*, which was released in 1946. The girls had a good old time on the set. As Barbara told Laura Wagner in *Films of the Golden Age* magazine decades later, "Peggy Ann had a very good sense of humor. We used to do a lot of wild things

Paired up again with pal Barbara Whiting in *Home Sweet Homicide*.

With her *Home Sweet Homicide* siblings, played by Dean Stockwell and Connie Marshall.

together. We were good pals. She was wonderful, and she was like a sister to me. She was generous and very loving, fun, never demanding. Never acted the movie star. We just sat around with our feet up and, you know, got in a little trouble." What kind of trouble? A *Modern Screen* interview seems to shed a bit of light on that. It seems that one time the girls decided to picket their *Junior Miss* director George Seaton during the noon hour "because Betty Grable and June Haver were glamour girls, yet Whiting and Garner

Peggy and Barbara form their own little picket line, much to the amusement of cast and crew. (From the collection of Laura Wagner)

couldn't be slick chicks." Their picket signed read "Geo Seaton and Bill Perlberg UNFAIR why Betty Grable instead of us."

Lighthearted trouble, for sure.

In what appears to be a Movie and Radio Critics press release from 1946, Peggy was again lauded. "Peggy Ann Garner was recently named the most outstanding Juvenile actress of 1945, according to a poll of motion picture and radio critics conducted by the *Film Daily*. This is considered to be the most representative poll in the industry." The two-page release ends "Peggy Ann lives with her mother in Beverly Hills, California, while her father Lt. William Garner is in Tokyo with the Army of Occupation."

Then came the night Peggy would remember for the rest of her life.

CHAPTER 7

March 7 was the night of the Academy Awards ceremony, held at Graumann's Chinese Theatre. Peggy wondered why she had been invited to this adult affair and given an aisle seat. The speeches had grown long and boring for the child until, lost in a daydream, she was jabbed in the ribs by her mother. It seems that emcee Bob Hope had just called out Peggy's name. There must be some mistake, she thought. Nevertheless, she was being literally pushed forward, so she advanced to the stage and was presented with a special Academy Award as the "Outstanding Child Performer of 1945." (Special Oscars were awarded to children, so that they were not competing with adults.) That miniature Oscar would mean the world to Virginia as the years progressed. It was validation of her hard work.

That night, Peggy took her Oscar to bed with her, as one would a cherished doll.

The next day, Peggy added the incoming mail to her scrapbook. Telegrams of congratulations were received from Richard Lyon, Grandma Craig, and Aunt Sota.

Peggy was now starting to spend a lot of time at the Whiting home. They, too, were living without a husband and father. Composer Richard Whiting had died when Barbara was only seven, so she understood Peggy's loneliness for her daddy. "My mother sort of mothered Peggy," says Barbara. "She drove her up to the prison all the time to see her mother." Peggy responded eagerly to the loving attention she was receiving from Mrs. Whiting, who was a woman with a strong religious background.

Outstanding Child Actress of 1945 — Peggy with her special Oscar.
(From the collection of the DeVito family)

Screen dad James Dunn won an Oscar that year, too. Other winners were Ray
Milland, Joan Crawford, and Anne Revere [From the collection of Mary Eckard]

"She was wonderful to my mother," continues Barbara, "and my mother was wonderful to her too."

Peggy and Barbara had so much fun together. "We laughed a lot, and I really felt there wasn't much laughter in her house at all." Sometimes they would go to the movies, sometimes to Ocean Park down at the beach. It was at the Whiting home that Peggy was finally in a true, honest-to-goodness family environment and enjoyed wonderful home cooking. "[Peggy, who loved nicknames] always called me 'Rabbit,'" said Barbara in the *Films of the Golden Age* interview with Laura Wagner. "First, it was Arabrab, Barbara backwards, but we shortened it to Rabbit. We called her Peggity."

Enjoying some at-home time, where she could kick back and just be a kid.
(From the collection of Connie Stratton)

Peggy and Barbara, best buddies. (From the collection of Laura Wagner)

It was here at the Whiting home that Peggy really began to blossom. Her first unchaperoned date was with Skip Rowland, the seventeen-year-old back who led UCLA to football victory over St. Mary's with the winning touchdown in November 1945. It's not difficult to figure out why Peggy decided she wanted to attend UCLA someday.

On March 10, 1946, Virginia was out of jail. She announced to the media that she had divorced William Garner in 1939 and was now married to Lt. Commander Theodore Trautwein of Hackensack, New Jersey, who was at sea on the U.S.S. Griggs. They had married in Tijuana, she said. (Tijuana records showed that Virginia Jeanne Timkin had married Theodore Walter Troutwein in January.)

Soon after reading this item in the newspaper, Bill Garner, who was now on General Douglas MacArthur's staff with the provost marshal in Tokyo, had Canton, Ohio lawyer Faber J. Drunkenbrod check the records. Drunkenbrod discovered that Bill had sued for divorce in 1939, asking for custody of Peggy, but the entire action had been dismissed. This meant that no divorce had taken place, making Virginia an unintentional bigamist.

Twentieth Century-Fox press agents hastened to fetch Virginia from the on-location site of Peggy's latest film and told her to give a statement to the media. After conferring with attorney Samuel A. Rosenthal, Virginia released a statement expressing her shock at the findings. If the Garners are not yet divorced, she said, she would get an annulment from Trautwein and a divorce from Garner. Once the final decree of divorce is received, she would then remarry Trautwein.

Garner was found to be correct. The divorce had not been finalized.

Virginia proceeded to have her second marriage annulled in Chihuahua, Mexico that July and reinstated the divorce process with Garner. She charged him with cruelty, telling the *L. A. Times:* "He was always using abusive language toward me. He called me a fool consistently. Once he became angry during a bridge game and began breaking up the furniture. He had me crying all the time and I became so nervous that I had to go to a sanitarium for 6 weeks."

The following year, the Garners' divorce was complete. They were given joint custody of Peggy, and the child would live with Virginia. Bill Garner, under a property agreement, would send Peggy one-dollar-per-month for her support and receive seven and one-half percent of her gross earnings in return.

With her fuzzy little friend. (From the collection of Connie Stratton)

Peggy loved charm bracelets. These were the ones she had in the 1940s.

The *L. A. Times* reported that Bill was now employed by the U.S. Department of Agriculture in New York City.

Virginia would be free to remarry Trautwein in twelve months, but she was having second thoughts about doing so. "I may not remarry Commander Trautwein after all," she told the *Herald Express*. "It will be a year before I get my final decree and anything can happen in a year." (If Virginia had yearned for a feeling of importance, she missed a golden opportunity. Mr. Trautwein would later become a prominent New Jersey judge.)

In the meantime, while pal Barbara was beginning a nine-year stretch as Peggy's *Junior Miss* character on radio, Peggy was gracing the cover of yet another popular magazine. Looking confident and very pretty, she appeared on the May 31, 1946 issue of *The Family Circle* magazine, complete with ribbons in her now-curly hair. According to the accompanying article, the reporter was surprised that fourteen-year-old Peggy had come to the interview alone. (This interview probably took place months before, while Virginia was still in jail.) Since she was able to interview Peggy directly, journalist Naomi Jolles learned what a poised young lady Peggy had become. It seemed she always said just the right thing, never blurting out anything for which she might have been sorry later. Peggy was a charming girl, with a cute light giggle, she reported. So unusual for a person of her age! She was never forced into the motion picture industry, Peggy told her. Her mother was willing to leave it anytime Peggy wanted to. She felt sorry for children whose mothers weren't as understanding as hers. The thing is that Peggy loved acting, she said. It was great fun.

The entertainment industry, the article explains, is fraught with fantasy and adulation. Peggy would get as many as six hundred letters a day from fans, and receive gifts from many of the people with whom she worked. Among gifts she received were an amethyst ring from director George Seaton, a gold bracelet from co-star Joan Blondell, and silver charms from many others. She now had four charm bracelets—two gold and two silver. If someone gave Peggy a gift, she insisted that an identical gift be given to her stand-in. When asked to describe someone in her life, regardless of whether that person was a world-famous star or a security officer, her favorite adjectives were "wonderful," "perfect," and "super." Such an upbeat, perky, happy child Peggy seemed to be!

In fact, Peggy was to present herself that way to reporters throughout her life. No matter how she truly felt, she was told to put on a happy face and behave as though everything was wonderful. If an injustice was done to her, she was to pretend it never happened. Only when she was playing a character was it acceptable for her to express negative emotions.

Reporters who wanted the unvarnished truth would have to go elsewhere to find it.

The public just couldn't get enough of Peggy and was clamoring for more. The Rexall drugstore chain published its

One of her favorite pastimes was reading mysteries.

own magazine each month, and a very attractive Peggy graced the cover of their back-to-school September 1946 issue. Inside was an article written by *The Rexall Magazine* Graphologist, in which a note from Peggy was shown and her handwriting was analyzed. Explaining which strokes indicated each character trait, he wrote that he found her to be a fun-loving, unspoiled girl who was also capable of serious thought. She was mentally balanced and showed much spiritual strength. Peggy had a "keen mind and an understanding heart," he

Peggy played boogie-woogie by ear.

said. Her loving, trusting nature made her vulnerable to being hurt as she tended to be somewhat gullible. He wrote that Peggy was able to find happiness in even small things. Her strokes indicated self-confidence, but a lack of vanity. She was a perfectionist in her work, doing what she could to make a project as good as it could be, which was more important to her than personal praise. She had a generous and sweet nature that endeared her to those around her. All this, he said, was evident in her handwriting.

While working at the studio, Peggy still spent three hours of each workday at the studio school. It was a lonely class, however, because there were just a few students there. As Barbara Whiting told writer Laura Wagner, "All you're doing during the day is just studying, and other than going out on the set to do your scenes, you don't have a social life. In regular high school there's always sports and things to get involved in . . . At the studio you weren't allowed to because not only did you have to learn your lines, you had to learn your English." Final exams were taken at the Los Angeles Board of Education building and took eight hours. Now Peggy's favorite subjects were English and history, but she did not like Latin or algebra at all. Nevertheless, she made excellent grades—A's in the subjects she liked and A minuses in those she didn't. Peggy asked her mother if she could go to public school so she wouldn't be so isolated. Her wish would soon be granted.

The media wanted to believe Peggy and Lon were seriously dating, but they were just pals.

Peggy's next film was *Daisy Kenyon*, in which she again played a young girl. How she yearned to play mature, sophisticated women. After all, she thought, she's fifteen whole years old now! Peggy would long remember that the picture's star, Joan Crawford, insisted that the set be kept freezing cold. It felt like being inside a refrigerator. Nevertheless, Peggy's enthusiastic personality quickly won over her co-stars and studio executives alike, and she was affectionately nicknamed "Mousemeat" by her peers. An energetic teen, she was unable to sit still for very long.

Peggy didn't know it at the time, but *Daisy Kenyon*, released in 1947, was to be her final picture for Twentieth Century-Fox in that decade.

At age fifteen, Peggy was now earning $1,500 per week and attending public school—University High in West Los Angeles. This school educated students from all walks of life. As for the future, Peggy had changed her mind about a college choice. She and her best friend Barbara hoped to someday attend Northwestern University together.

Virginia was strict about many things. She would not allow her daughter to wear jeans or sloppy shirts, and neither could Peggy go on solo dates, but she *was* able to participate in dances and football games, just as regular kids did. The problem, though, was that the other students had not been very accepting of her at first. Peggy Ann Garner was a screen princess, after all, and they assumed she would be snobbish. Boys thought she must be accustomed to much better places than they could afford.

In April, the press began speculating that there was a romance going on between Peggy and eighteen-year-old Viscount Anthony Furness, heir to a six-million-dollar shipbuilding fortune, because he had sent Peggy his regimental insignia. The next day, Viscount Furness responded that there was no romance. It was "just a beautiful friendship, and marriage is quite out of the question."

Co-starring again with Lon McCallister in *Bob, Son of Battle.*

No romance, perhaps, but Peggy was loved by many. A sketch by the popular cartoonist Frank Miller appeared in print on May 8, 1947. It was run as a tribute from an artist who had much admiration for Peggy.

Modern Screen ran a very nice article about Peggy in October 1947. Included were many delightful photos of her with her friends—Barbara Whiting, Harry Macy, Betty Sullivan, Scotty Beckett, and many others. They were having a wonderful time at this party, one that was thought to have been the result of Virginia's motherly love for Peggy and her efforts to help her classmates warm up to her. "Every Friday night is open house at the Garners' pleasant middle-sized home," the article states, "and the neighborhood kids pour in for parties that bend the walls." Records and radio provided the music for dancing, games provided the fun, and Mom provided

Peggy could sell anything. (From the collection of Peter Kasimatis)

the Cokes and sandwiches, it said. In reality, however, the festivities pictured were taking place at Barbara's house, not Peggy's. Harry Macy was the Whitings' neighbor and friend, so he was invited to their frequent parties, as was Peggy. Misrepresenting the source of these get-togethers to *Modern Screen* was the studio's attempt to protect Peggy from the negative publicity caused by her mother's many run-ins with the law.

Peggy enjoyed her friends, loved being around them. It didn't take long for her bubbly personality to win over her more timid classmates, and dates with regular, everyday boys from both University High and Beverly Hills High eventually resulted.

Peggy enjoyed doing the routine things that regular kids took for granted. She was a football fan and went to many high school and college games. The boys in her life were many—Tony, David, Harry, Bud, Sir Charles, John, and Mitch were a few of them.

Every now and then, newspapers and magazines would speculate that she was seriously dating this celebrity or that. In an issue of *Movie Life*, for instance, she is pictured putting a boutonniere on her *Thunder in the Valley* co-star, Lon McCallister, with loving looks being exchanged. This is listed in their index under the heading "Romance in the News." The truth, however, was that those things were done merely for publicity purposes, while most of the boys she truly dated were not as well known. Lon was nicknamed "Buddy Mack" by Peggy and Barbara and they were all very good friends, but there was no romance involved. Nine years older than Peggy, Lon looked much younger than he was and had given Peggy her first screen kiss in *Thunder in the Valley*, so the media had felt that they would be the perfect couple. Consequently, they would often present them as such, regardless of the facts.

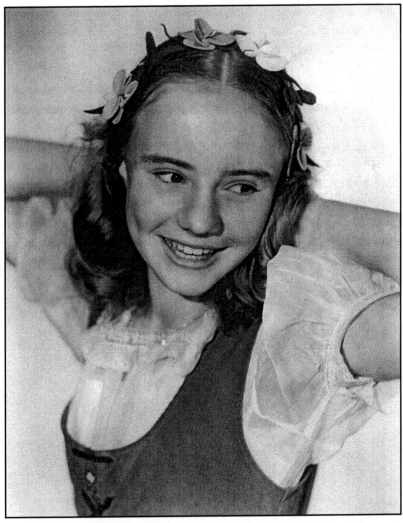

Ever feminine, ever gentle was Peggy. (From the collection of Connie Stratton)

Peggy and William Anthony Viscount Furness were still an item too, according to *Motion Picture* magazine. From his home in England, it said, he would write and phone her frequently. While they were both in New York, he took her to the Champagne Room at El Morocco. At Christmastime, he sent her flowers and an embroidered evening purse. "He's just another pal," Peggy reassured the reporter.

Once filming was complete, Peggy appeared in a magazine ad for Royal Crown Cola, which was also used to plug *Thunder in the Valley*.

Consideration for others had always been one of Peggy's strong points.

She took drama in high school, but didn't try out for parts in the plays that were presented. That would be showing off, she felt, and wouldn't be fair to the other students.

She had always been a creative person, too. When Peggy didn't have a film in which to express it, she would write short stories and poems. While she admitted this to reporters, she didn't feel that her creations were good enough for them to see.

Peggy had a driver's license now and would sometimes be allowed to drive her mother's new black Buick. Other times, she was driven by others. Dick Haymes, for instance, took Peggy and Barbara to Romanoff's for dinner, then to the circus one day. As Barbara said in *Films of the Golden Age*, "I liked Dick Haymes, he was a family friend. He used to take me and Peggy Ann Garner, because we were all at Fox, to Ocean Park. He was very fatherly toward Peggy and myself." The girls so enjoyed those excursions.

CHAPTER 8

Facing eviction from the Canon Drive home, Peggy and Virginia petitioned the court for permission to buy the house at 2907 Motor Avenue. Lawyers from Twentieth Century-Fox and the bank were in attendance. The judge asked those representing the studio if they felt there was any reason in the future that they would drop Peggy, and they assured him there was not. Peggy's earnings were now $1,250 per week. Permission to buy the house was granted. Citizens Trust & Savings Bank, which had control of Peggy's funds, was authorized to pay $20,000 down and $150 per month until the note was paid in full.

Now that permission was theirs, Virginia and Peggy didn't buy the Motor Avenue house. Instead, they purchased the one at 201 S. Bentley Avenue.

This home was large enough that Peggy now had a bedroom of her own for what was said to be the first time in her life. On the small table in her room was displayed her most treasured possession—her Oscar. On the walls were pin-up photos of her screen heroes—Lon McCallister, Dick Haymes, Bill Eythe, and Peter Lawford. And she had a new dog now, a golden cocker spaniel pup named "Miss Skitch."

One of Peggy's scrapbook entries during this time was a note from actor Peter Lawford that must have caused her heart to skip a beat or two from excitement. It said, "Peggy—You're looking awful cute today! Why don't you come and visit me on Stage 8 after lunch? Peter." How envious his fans would have been of Peggy's easy access to their idol!

Peggy was being given the royal treatment these days—she rode in the World War II victory parade for General Eisenhower, and was a guest

The house Peggy and Virginia bought, on Bentley. This is how it looks today.
(From the collection of Jeff Howard)

Peggy's growing up. Note her perfume collection and Lon McCallister photo
in the background.

A moment of relaxation. (From the collection of Connie Stratton)

of the Trumans at the White House, being given the honor of sitting next to the fascinating Eleanor Roosevelt. More photo spreads of Peggy showed up in movie magazines, showing her fans what a fun, down-to-earth, teenager she was.

Virginia was ecstatic for her daughter. And, for being Peggy's mother and getting her to the studio on time, she was given a salary of $1,000 per month. Virginia's happiness was hard won—and short-lived.

Mrs. Garner's propensity for personal drama and her weakness for the bottle were spotlighted in major newspapers for the world to see. It was an embarrassment for her daughter and the studio.

Then the film industry changed dramatically.

CHAPTER 9

The motion-picture business was slowing down. Perhaps this was because the studio executives foresaw a big change that would be happening in the industry soon. An antitrust ruling would come down in May 1948 that would break up the studios' close association with individual theaters. Until then, the studios had been assured that certain theaters would favor their productions and, thus, they would be pretty much guaranteed some degree of success. That would no longer be the case. Consequently, Peggy's option, along with that of many other actors, was not renewed. Many contract players were now out on the streets.

Nevertheless, Virginia was sent a script for the proposed film entitled *Bomba, the Jungle Boy*. This picture was to be shot by Monogram in six days. For this, Peggy would be paid $8,000. Virginia felt that it was beneath Peggy to do such a film, so she flatly rejected it.

In August, Virginia went to Edward D. Dibs in Beverly Hills and asked him to be their business manager. Their business association was purely verbal, she claimed, and no contract was signed. She later wrote,

> **It was due to the business affairs becoming more than I felt I was capable of handling that I had consulted and retained Mr. Dibs [*not his real name,* ed.]…When a man in this capacity is hired, one turns over all business to him and relates any and all confidential matters. Therefore, I related to Mr. Dibs the situation of my arrest in a check charge of many years back. I did this as a protection, as I had done with my studio.**
>
> **To begin with, to get our affairs in order, his service charge**

would be $2,500.00. This I agreed on. Other than this, he was entitled to only 5% of the income in the picture industry.

A few days after he had been retained, he put before me a proposition in which he stated he could save me more money in taxes than I could ever afford to pay him. His plan was along the lines of a corporation. I advised him he could not incorporate where a minor was concerned and the court would hold jurisdiction. He said he felt he could get by the court, as he planned to use a retired judge in Beverly Hills whom he felt could sway the court...I then told him he also had the bank to contend with as they were guardian of the estate. He said he would have projection sheets drawn and submit some to the bank. This was done. The bank took the stand they would remain neutral and leave it up to the court. It was then decided to have the contracts drawn...Meeting in [the retired judge's] office, the figures were discussed and Dibs advised me I would need another lawyer. [The retired judge] would represent the company to be formed, to be known as Excello. I wanted to call Irving Bishop, who was my attorney, had been for many years and also represented the bank. Dibs said no, he wanted to use one of his own lawyers, who was just around the corner...[Dibs' lawyer] was called and a few minutes later was in the office. He was quickly briefed and was advised he would be representing Peggy and I...This interview broke up and I was advised they would send me the contracts in about ten days. The very next morning in the mail, I received a bill from [Dibs' lawyer] for $2,500.00 for services rendered. I was astounded and called Mr. Dibs. [Dibs' lawyer] had done nothing but put in an appearance. [The retired judge] was drawing the contracts. Mr. Dibs advised me to pay no attention to this bill, it was just a dummy for tax purposes. Right then and there, I smelled a rat and decided that Dibs was a crook...

A few days later, I received the finished contracts on Excello. This was a personal holding company and was headed by one Edward D. Dibs and a Mr. Russell Fisher, a man I had never heard of. Neither my daughter nor I were any part of this company. And at the time my daughter's production salary was $5,000 per week. The terms of this contract were Excello would put her under personal contract at $100.00 per week. This would be all she was to pay personal taxes on. She would become a loan out to Excello from her studio, her studio salary being paid into the company, and they would take 50%. Other terms in this contract sold my daughter lock, stock and barrel to this company.

I on my own would never sign such a contract. The bank also would have heavily opposed such a set up. I told Mr. Dibs I would have to send the contract to Peggy's father and let him also look over it. Even though we were divorced, I always consulted her father where any dealings were concerned regarding her affairs. Frankly, I never bothered—I knew I would not sign same. Over a period of several weeks, Dibs was after me to sign. I stalled by telling him I had not heard from Mr. Garner.

I was aware Mr. Dibs would never give me a release from our verbal agreement of his being our business manager, and I was greatly concerned. I was pretty certain he would want a large amount of money to be released from his bonds. Everything we had was under his control and I had no way of getting any funds unless I could somehow borrow them, and this would have to be paid back out of monies all owed me by court as her guardian—and Dibs was controlling this.

Why Virginia thought a verbal agreement was that binding is unknown. She wanted out, though, so she came up with a scheme that she thought might end her association with Dibs:

While in the Dibs office in New York, I was introduced to Hal Pierce, known as a Broadway Producer. He immediately wanted to know if Peggy Ann would or could be available for a Broadway show. I said that would depend entirely on the script—the part and the backing—and I wanted him to know her salary was high and I didn't think Broadway would pay it. He said the part was a lead. It was a musical and was backed by Robert C. Young, the railroad magnate. The show was titled *Greenbrier* and was [set] at White Sulphurs—Greenbrier Hotel. This sounded interesting. I read the script that day and was pleased. Then I gave him my figure for salary, plus expenses and teacher's salary. That night he delivered an Equity contract to me at the

Waldorf Astoria Hotel, complete with my demands. I advised him the studio, our agent and business manager would have to approve same. He said fine—take it to the coast and then airmail it back. We were due in New York for rehearsals in ten days.

This was like a dream from heaven. With this contract, I certainly would not need the loan. It would bring us to New York and I would be away from Dibs, and I was sure my troubles were over. I remained in New York for another day and forfeited the loan.

That afternoon, Peggy Ann called me saying she was to report to Monogram to work in the picture *Bomba, the Jungle Boy*. I advised Peggy to do no such thing. I was leaving that night and would be home the next day.

When I returned, I learned Peggy was at Monogram Studio, working. I called her agents. They said yes, Mr. Dibs had negotiated the contract. To the studio I went and found Peggy emoting before the camera. I asked the producer to see her contract. Who had signed it and was it court approved? He said Mr. Dibs handled everything. I advised the producer, Walter Murish, Peggy would not be on the set the next morning. He said she had to be; her salary had been paid in advance. From there, I went to Mr. Dibs. He had been paid and already had banked her check to her accounts. The next day, Peggy returned to school, not the studio. By ten o'clock that morning, I had half of Monogram at my home. If I didn't present her to finish the picture, they threatened to blackball me with every studio. She had been paid. Finally, so as not to hurt her, I let her finish the picture.

Having the adults who were in authority over her, pulling her in opposite directions, was quite distressing to Peggy. But at least life on the set was nice.

"We were young and had a lot of fun working together," says the film's star, Johnny Sheffield. "Peg Ann was an experienced actress and a true professional! She was on time, hit her marks, found her light, and knew her lines. This is important when you are working fast on a budget. It was no problem for Peggy." John, like many others, found her buoyant and cheerful, whether the camera was running or not.

He laughingly recalls one specific scene of this film: "I'll never forget

With Johnny Sheffield in *Bomba, the Jungle Boy*. (From the collection of
Johnny Sheffield)

the reading of her line 'Very cozy' in the scene where I was showing her
my cave digs and showing her where I expected her to stay. She didn't go
for it and Bomba had to build a shelter outside for her. I did manage to
get her into a well-tailored leopard skin!" That jungle boy Bomba would
just happen to have an outfit her size is where suspension of disbelief
comes in. This was a delightful film for old and young alike.

"I will always love and remember Peg Ann," he says. "It doesn't take
long to recognize the talents of a real trouper."

**The $8,000.00 salary, we never did see and the contract
had never been approved by court.**

Virginia knew better days were ahead. She and Peggy would soon be
going to New York to do a play that seemed wonderful.

**I had taken the Equity contracts to the studio, to her agents
and to Mr. Dibs. In each case, it was thought this was a fine**

contract and [they] advised me to sign it. Mr. Dibs did say he would ask yet for rehearsal money and the traveling and expense money in advance. He called Mr. Pierce in New York and this was granted, and riders were sent out to be attached to the contracts.

We were scheduled to arrive in New York on the following Sunday. On Friday, when I had not received the expense check, I went to Dibs' office to see if he had. Nothing had arrived, and while I was sitting in his office, Mr. Pierce called from New York. He claimed he had been so busy he had forgotten to go to the bank and get the money off. The banks were now closed. He could do nothing before Monday, and publicity stunts were arranged for our arrival Sunday a.m. and would we please come on and be there without fail. He would reimburse us first thing Monday. He told Dibs he had two checks in his pockets, one for $240,000.00 signed by Robert Young and one for $75,000.00 signed by Libby Holman Smith. Mr. Dibs told him to go to the law office of Max Chopnick on East 46th. When he got there to call us back. A few minutes later he did call back. Mr. Chopnick confirmed the fact he had these two checks. Dibs told Chopnick if Pierce would give him the $75,000.00 check to hold as security, he would let us come into New York as per schedule Sunday. To this point, I had still been able to stall Dibs on signing his Excello contract, saying Mr. Garner had not returned it.

Mr. Pierce met Peggy, her teacher, and I at the airport in New York. All publicity was handled and we settled in our hotel to start rehearsals on Wednesday. Pierce was to see me before to give me the expense money. He called during the week, each time saying how rushed he was, but I did not see him. Figuring Mr. Chopnick was holding the security, I did not worry. But the following Monday, I became concerned. Mr. Pierce had not showed up. There was no answer at his phone. I then went to Mr. Chopnick. He still had the $75,000.00 check in his drawer. At this point, it was sent to the bank to be certified. The check was found to be bogus. Mr. Chopnick told me not to worry, he would handle everything. I said no, realizing how lax he had been. I would find

Pierce. It took me three days, but with the help of a cab driver, I found him in the slum section of New York. The cab driver and I took him to the hotel and the hotel detectives took him to our suite. There, he confessed he was no producer, but an escapee from Bellevue Hospital. This was found to be true.

(How this was verified, Virginia did not say. She had been introduced to him by the Leonard Dibs Agency, an agency that is known for its prestige and integrity, now as much as ever. Why would they have had dealings with such a man? Why would Pierce have gone with her to her hotel?)

There was nothing I could do to the man; he was insane. We were simply out the monies involved for travel and living expenses. However, this did put a liability on our agents as an agent is liable for payment on all contracts. His duty was to have checked with Equity to make certain bond was posted for this production. The Equity forms Mr. Pierce had used had been stolen.

As a result of the position the agents were in, they advised I remain in New York a few days and they would try and find a play for Peggy. They came up with a script on a story called *Pick-Up Girl*. This was the worst piece of trash I had ever read. The story dealt with a young girl who became involved with a 40-year-old man and contracted syphilis. While this paid a good salary and been a hit on the London stage, I could not see my daughter of 15 years old in such a play, and I flatly refused to let her do it. Peggy's father arrived on the scene and he read the script. He said it was good for the theater and, since it paid so well, Peggy should do it. I was in a bad position: If I returned to the coast, I had Dibs to fight and this, I knew, was a bad situation. So after much argument in New York and with Mr. Garner over the play, we agreed to sign for the road tour. It would provide income Dibs would have no control over and would give me time to work out an amiable out with him.

CHAPTER 10

Rehearsals for the play *Pick-Up Girl* began in early 1948. Peggy practiced the play in stock at Reading, Pennsylvania, before they hit the road. Her education would be uninterrupted; tutor Alice "Steppy" Stepanian traveled with them.

Two weeks later, the play *Pick-Up Girl* opened in Washington, D.C. The play was fried. Peggy's performance given credit but I, as her mother, was again criticized in the public eye for permitting a talented child like this to do such a piece of trash. When I saw these reviews, I was brokenhearted. I couldn't see Peggy going on in this play. Leaving her in the hands of her teacher, I went to New York and tried to get out of the contract. Here, I was told I would have to confer with the producer. Back to Washington I went. With him, I could get nowhere. The following week, we opened in Philadelphia. The reviews ranted the same way; I was taking the criticism. I again appealed to the producer and he would do nothing, saying I should talk to my agents on the west coast. I flew to California to talk to them. They said I had to remain or be in trouble with Equity. Then I went to Equity in New York and they advised me I could give a two-week notice after the first 6 weeks. I returned to the producer and advised him of my intentions.

This resulted in a February 19, 1948 letter being sent to the Sam Jaffe Agency by Actors' Equity Association that said they had advanced Virginia $2,000 after seeing the telegram Virginia had signed that agreed to a run-of-play contract for Peggy. They also said the check had been cashed. Now Virginia was saying that she didn't send the telegram, the Sam Jaffe Agency did. "We must therefore inform you that if the Sam Jaffe Agency, acting under authority from Mrs. Garner, sent this telegram, we will insist that Mrs. Garner sign a Run-of-the Play contract. If however, the Jaffe Agency sent this telegram without authority, Equity will hold the Sam Jaffe Agency completely responsible."

The next four weeks, nobody received their salary; and in Toledo, Ohio, I broke up the show by pulling Peggy from the cast. I had no recourse but to return to California. I had signed our hotel bills and I had to take care of business. These I returned to Mr. Dibs. He at once told me of the bills to be paid, etc., but said he was paying nothing until his contract was signed. I finally told him I had no intention of filing or signing his contract on Excello. If he wanted to prepare a decent and fair contract, then it might be different. Mr. Dibs advised me he had exposed his hand to me…My reply to him was if he was big enough to go ahead, and with this I left his office.

I was in a desperate position. Unless I relied on Dibs for living expenses, as everything was now under his control, I had no means for support.

Apparently, Virginia did not see getting a job of her own, instead of depending on Peggy to support her, to be a viable option.

I tried to contact the man in New York where I had negotiated the loan prior to the episode with Mr. Pierce. Learning he had gone to Europe, I asked for a loan from his agents, against forthcoming salaries. This was rejected as all clients were asking the same thing, due to the industry being generally quiet, resulting from the beginning of TV. I appealed to the bank to have funds released from trust to carry us. An order was granted here to carry us a few weeks. However, this was limited because the cash in the estate had been pretty well used. We had just bought the home and the furnishings. Peggy was not working and no money was going in. Enough had to be kept on hand for insurance, mortgage, taxes, etc. Between Mr. Garner and my parents, we were able to carry on a few more weeks, but our overhead was high.

Perhaps that was because Virginia enjoyed staying at pricey hotels. Too, she had bought Peggy a car of her own, a breezy tan 1947 Ford convertible.

> I sold some things, hocked others, mortgaged the cars and furniture, and a while longer we got by. Dibs [was] constantly riding and fighting me over his contract and the bills to be paid. The creditors were driving him mad, threatening to blackball us...
>
> Well aware this could hurt us in the public eye, I still did not sign. To do so would hurt Peggy much more.
>
> As time went on, we lost our cars and the things I had hocked.

How distressing this must have been to Peggy! Not only was it embarrassing, but she loved her car.

Peggy had received excellent tutoring, and she was now a high school junior with high marks in English, French, Spanish, psychology, and history. Outdoor sports still attracted Peggy like a magnet; indoors, she would play hit records. When asked who her favorite actress was, she would

With Susan Peters in *The Sign of the Ram*. (From the collection of Laura Wagner)

Frank Worth Photo for QUICK

Poor Shot: Peggy Ann Garner (left) tries to squirt whipped cream on Elizabeth Taylor's banana split, hits Elizabeth instead, misses young actor Dick Clayton. Scene of this candid picture is a teen-age, movie-star party given by Jane Powell at the opening of her father's new "malt shop" in Hollywood.

Oops! (*Quick* magazine)

reply without hesitation, "Barbara Stanwyck." She, of course, didn't know it then but someday she would find herself working with her idol.

Peggy did two pictures during this time.

She appeared in the Columbia film, *The Sign of the Ram*. During the off times while technicians were adjusting the lighting or other such delays were happening on the set, Peggy could be found off to the side, knitting. This had become one of her favorite pastimes. Reporters had spotted her knitting argyle socks on the set and asked whom they were for. Peggy admitted she was making them for a boyfriend, but stopped short of giving them his name.

Once the film had wrapped, she then helped promote it by appearing in a two-page *Photoplay* spread in March 1948, modeling clothes and plugging the film.

Now Peggy was finally able to go back to University High. She threw a much-publicized party at home with dancing, feasting on hotdogs and other teen favorites, and much gaiety. Invited were her friends from school and only one other movie star—after all, no party would be complete for Peggy without her best friend, Barbara.

In the August 1948 issue of *Movie Teen* was a four-page picture-story of Peggy, Kathleen Hughes, Peggy Egertson, Sandra McMillan and Joan Whilhart enjoying a festive pajama party at Lois Butler's house. In this apparently staged party being recorded by cameraman Frank Worth, Peggy was pictured being greeted at the door, brushing Lois' hair, listening in on another girl's telephone conversation (as were the other four girls), listening to records, toasting weenies and drinking Coke, acting out "a left-handed Indian" in a game of Charades that had everyone laughing, participating in the songfest as Lois and Joan played the piano, and sound

With *The Big Cat* co-star, Lon McCallister.

asleep in the giant bed with the other five girls. This was a cute, light-hearted article that Peggy's fans would love.

Soon she was cast in the Eagle-Lion film *The Big Cat*, which was filming on location in Utah. Her co-star Lon McCallister fondly remembers working with her in this picture. "Peggy Ann was a perfect leading lady and I loved her," he says. This would be Peggy's first romantic role, so it was a real plus having her good friend Lon as her leading man.

So comfy was their relationship that it resulted in a bit of mischief. Peggy had sneaked into Lon's room one day and put salt all over his bed. He later discovered this naughty deed and laughed it off, but the joke ended up being on Peggy. The very next day, Lon waited until Peggy was elsewhere, then sneaked over to her room and put water in *her* bed.

Some publicity was given to *The Big Cat* when Peggy appeared on the cover of the July issue of *Movie Teen* and inside was a mention of her latest film. She and Lon also appeared together in a magazine ad for Tangee lipstick, which also plugged the film.

Mention of the film was made, too, in a *Movie Stars Parade* article found in the February 1949 issue. Entitled "It's a Date," this article takes its readers along on Peggy's roller-skating date with Scotty Beckett, who had worked with her in *Junior Miss* four years earlier. At the beginning of this picture-story, Scotty is waiting on the sofa of her home as Peggy gets ready. Tacked onto the wall directly behind the sofa is a UCLA pennant.

Mr. Dibs, both times, got the money and yet would pay no bills. One will never know the mental anguish I suffered, the heartache and embarrassment I went through. Our phone was even disconnected, but still I would not sell Peggy out.

Soon, Peggy was off again. This time she went east for an eight-week run of *Kiss and Tell*.

While other people thought her freckles were cute, Peggy didn't like them at all, so she covered them with make-up. She revealed this little trick to Mary Jane Fulton, who wrote the "Beauty Spots" feature article in *Photoplay*. In their March 1949 issue, Peggy also shared with readers her method of maintaining moist skin when she was working in a dry climate.

In March of 1949, the offer came of the very fine play *Peg O' My Heart*. This would pay us $1,250.00 per week and was

to be a road tour, starting in June. This was an ideal role and Peggy was perfect for the part, now being 17 years old. I was so happy and so was Peggy. If somehow we could hold out another four months. She would also be graduating in June.

I leased my [Peggy's] house furnished and was able to get six months rent in advance. Still under the wing of Dibs, I had to have him draw the lease. The six months rent was paid to him, and he did pay three months rent on a furnished apartment for us to live in and now provided eating money and nothing else. He was aware the payments had to be made on our furniture when he accepted the six months rent and agreed to make same.

Even though Peggy's good friend B had moved away, they still kept in touch. Once, B came to Hollywood to meet with Peggy for a day of shopping. After they were done with their shopping, they took a Greyhound bus to B's house. This had all been okayed earlier when B's aunt cleared it through Virginia. The girls had a marvelous time, and even went out on a double date. Peggy's date was a boy named Ray, a very nice boy who was highly respected by his classmates. So taken was Peggy by Ray that they dropped B and her date off early and spent the next six hours together, talking. When she finally got back to B's house, Peggy was floating on air. She just adored Ray. At daybreak, police appeared at the door. Virginia had reported her daughter missing, as either a victim of kidnappers or a runaway. The girls were mortified. To ease Virginia's mind, B's mother drove Peggy back home right away.

Soon she was back to work with a role in *The Loveable Cheat*. Richard Ney co-starred in that production and recalls, "Peggy Ann Garner was not only lovely but also full of laughter and a source of joy to everyone."

A film entitled *Home of the Brave* had been released in 1949 and its producer, Stanley Kramer, had been scheduled to receive a citation from the Anti-Defamation League. Kramer couldn't make it to the ceremony, however, so they asked Peggy to appear with the film's star, James Edwards, to receive the citation for him. She happily obliged.

Peggy was also doing some radio work. These were very busy years for Peggy and she was making lots of friends on the set, but most of her film salary went to pay creditors for her mother's past debts. In spite of all this work and its resulting income, she was unable to keep up the payments on her house, and it was put up for sale.

With Charlie Ruggles in *The Lovable Cheat*. (From the collection of Laura Wagner)

Peggy's high school career was almost at its end. She had served on University High's Friendship Board this final year and enjoyed the social aspects of school but, even though she made good grades, she had less-fond feelings about academics. On May 4, 1949, she wrote a letter to a friend named Mitch, who was attending Stanford University:

> First, apologies for not answering your letter sooner, but honest injun, I've been busy! First, I don't have to tell you, being a Senior keeps you kinda busy! 2nd, I went to Salt Lake City last week for the opening of a picture. We had quite a busy time. Saw Bill and Herbie Hustand, and lent them a shoulder to cry on, as they are kinda lonely for good old California. I can't say I blame them. This is the only place.
>
> School goes on as usual. They're finally painting the old place, just as we graduate naturally. We have been given earthquake instructions, in case it should come, and everyone thinks it's going to be a whopper. Hmm, I may hop a jet and head for Northern California.
>
> How's good old Stanford? Busy as ever I guess. When will

you be home for vacation? Hope I get to see you Mitch—it's been a long time, and I mean it seriously.

The weather has been beautiful. Just perfect enough to set my little mind to work figuring out legitimate ways to ditch and head for the beach. I've turned into a regular delinquent—going off bounds for lunch and everything. But I'm getting kinda cautious, as ye olde diploma time is too close to risk losing!

Well, gotta get back to my homework, so till soon—

> be good Mitch
> and please write
> soon and often, huh?

> Love as ever
> Peggy

Peggy graduated from University High School at the age of seventeen, honored by her peers for being the "Best Thespian" and "Girl With the Best Complexion." Virginia was heartbroken that she couldn't afford to buy her a graduation gift. When she saw Peggy's class picture, tears came to her eyes. Her dear daughter was the only one there who did not have a class sweater. Why didn't she ask for one, Virginia wondered. Peggy explained that she knew how distressed her mother had been about their meager money situation and didn't want to worry her further.

During the summer, Peggy was signed to appear in *Junior Miss* in summer stock in Barnesville, Pennsylvania. Then she was to tour the States for five weeks in *Peg O' My Heart*. It was this play that would change Peggy's life forever.

CHAPTER 11

When the contracts were negotiated for the tour of *Peg O' My Heart*, to open in Chicago, Dibs again had to handle this as the business manager, and it was through the Leonard Dibs Agency. I had ordered Peggy's wardrobe for the play and we were all ready to leave. I went to the offices of Leonard Dibs, our agent. It was understood I was going to have to take an advance on Peggy's salary for our expenses and her wardrobe. And I went to pick this up. This was the day before our scheduled departure. I was advised Mr. Ed Dibs had made other arrangements and I would have to see him.

When I approached Ed Dibs, he said he would give me nothing. I was not going on this tour. Peggy was grown up. She had just graduated, she knew the business and she could get along. Nothing would happen to her. Whatever wardrobe she needed she could get when she got there. And anything else, she could call him. I told him I thought he must be crazy. I wouldn't think of letting her go alone. A 17-year-old girl on the road alone in show business. I asked him if he wasn't aware of the hazards that could come to her. He advised me he had talked to Peggy and asked her if she thought she would be all right on her own. Her reply had been yes. But what teenager wouldn't delight in traveling alone and feel they were grown up? He advised me he had booked all her hotels and transportation as single only, and he was taking full responsibility. This was done through the Revel Travel Bureau and is a matter of record. He flatly refused to even provide a ticket for me. And if I went, he told me he would have the hotel association after me for unpaid bills that were still owing from the tour of *Pick-Up Girl*. He said they would make it hot for me. I advised him I was sure when they knew why the bills had not been paid, they would work with me on a fair basis. I had nothing to run away from or fear. I told him I would agree to pay them so much out of each week's salary when we were on the road and keep all current bills paid. He still refused to issue my transportation. Peggy had to leave that night as she was due in Chicago for rehearsal and bound to a contract. He gave me her ticket and travel money for her and told me it was up to me to see to it she was there.

Peggy was looking forward to traveling alone, seeing it as a lark. "Mama, just give me a chance to show you—I'll be good," Peggy pleaded. "It would be so much fun going alone. Since you didn't give me anything for graduation, let this be my present."

It so happened our neighbors were going out on the same train, and I asked them to look after Peggy. Then I wired friends of many years standing to meet her in Chicago and to take her to her hotel and look after her until I could get there a few days later. The next day, I went to the law office of Charles Katz and had a petition drawn revoking any and all agreements between Mr. Dibs and I, and as of that day his services were terminated.

Virginia's public image was taking a beating. Two days after the tour had begun, a columnist had written, "Peggy Ann Garner headed east for summer stock, 'soloing'—Mamma, isn't she a little young for this?" Yes, Virginia felt she was *definitely* too young for this, but it seemed she had little say in the matter.

I went to Mr. Bach at the Citizens National Trust department and explained my troubles. I had to join my child and get her wardrobe which had been ordered for the play. I need $1,250.00 and if the trust department would advance same and I would repay it out of earnings from the road tour. Mr. Bach was only a trust officer and could not grant the request

Pretty Peggy. (From the collection of Connie Stratton)

without court approval or the approval of [illegible] who was on vacation. I left the bank in tears, fearful for my child.

That night, I went to friends in Beverly Hills, Mr. and Mrs. Charlie Hoffritz, with my troubles. Charlie gave me $1,250.00 and called over his manager, a Mr. Ward Farrow. Charlie briefed Mr. Farrow and told him to go with me the next day to Dibs and ask to see his books. Whatever Dibs wanted, Charlie would pay, and Ward Farrow would then straighten out our affairs on an honest and fair basis.

The next day, Farrow and I did go to Dibs and Mr. Farrow asked to see the books on the Garner account. Dibs said his books were not open to anybody. Mr. Farrow then asked how much he wanted to turn the account over. He said it was not for sale. At this time, he claimed he had not as yet received any legal paper terminating his services. From there, Mr. Farrow and I went up to the Sam Jaffe Agency on Sunset, who were Peggy's picture agents. We talked to Phil Gersh and advised him Dibs was no longer our manager. Mr. Farrow was going to take over and the agency was to have no further dealing with Dibs. A letter was left on file verifying this, prior to our departure.

In front of the Jaffe Agency, Mr. Farrow gave me a check for $2,000.00, told me to pay what was urgent, and for the time being to quit worrying about Dibs; for me to get to Chicago and my child, where I was needed. We would straighten all this out when we returned from the tour. Besides Mr. Farrow's check, I had Charlie Hoffritz' for $1,250.00. Later that day, I picked up Peggy's wardrobe, paid what I knew were pressing bills, got my ticket and deposited $800.00 to my checking account in the Pico Branch of the Citizen's National Bank. That night I left for Chicago, where I joined my child.

Before going out to the suburb where Peggy was, I went directly from the train to the main office of the Hotel Association. Here, I talked to John Coon, the man who had sent me such threatening letters regarding our delinquent bills. When this man learned the trouble I had had, he said, "Mrs. Garner, you never gave us any trouble." It was this guy Dibs who had consistently given him the runaround. [He] advised me Mr. Dibs had blackened me unmercifully to creditors and said he was no credit to Peggy or I in representing us. This man couldn't have been nicer to me and told me when I got to the hotel where Peggy was to disregard the letter that would be handed to me on arrival. I paid Mr. Coon $100.00 and agreed to pay so much weekly on the old bills. He called the hotel before I left and told them to be nice to me—I was a pretty nice person, I had simply had a rough time.

When I registered at the hotel, I was informed they did not have an adjoining room to Peggy's. I said never mind another room; I would go in with Peggy. The clerk said he was sorry, but Peggy's accommodation had been booked through a travel

A page of Peggy's scrapbook, captioned "Chicago — 'Peg O' My Heart' – summer – 1949." (From the collection of Jeff Howard)

bureau for single only and he could not change the order and the bill to be paid by them. This I could not change either.

Virginia then went to the theatre to see her daughter. When she entered Peggy's dressing room, however, she discovered a boy in there with her. One of Virginia's greatest fears was that Peggy would succumb to wanton Hollywood ways and become pregnant without benefit of matrimony. Her fear turned into irrational behavior and she accused Peggy often of being pregnant. This was one of those times.

This not only embarrassed Peggy, but it also made her feel that she wasn't trusted and her mother was interfering in her life. She, understandably, became very upset. This is how she explained it to Dick Moore, as he quotes her in his 1984 book *Twinkle, Twinkle, Little Star*: "God knows how many times I was accused of being pregnant. I don't know how that could have happened, unless somebody phoned it in. She always put the fear of God in me, about anything and everything. I didn't even know how you got pregnant, but she'd have me convinced that I was. And this fear, I'm sure, followed me when I grew to be an adult and when I got married."

Thoroughly embarrassed, Peggy left in a huff with the boy, leaving her mother alone.

It's natural, during their adolescent years, for young people to be rebellious and to have love-hate feelings for their parents. For Peggy, those feelings were further intensified by the topsy-turvy showbiz world in which she lived, and complicated by the conflicting feedback she was getting from people who were in authority over her. Her agent was urging Peggy to pay no attention to Virginia, as was her father.

Ten days later when the show closed in Chicago, I went to the producer to pick up Peggy's check. He advised me her contract read checks to be sent to Edward Dibs in California. This order had been attached by rider to the contract. I said I was Peggy's guardian and I was requesting this check. Mr. Meggs advised me he knew how I felt but he would be in violation of Equity and subject to fine if he paid it to me. Not wanting trouble, I said very well, I would straighten the matter out with the Leonard Dibs Agency. I called them on the coast that night but couldn't reach them. Then I called Dibs. This was the first he was aware I was east. I told him he need not be concerned about the hotel association bothering me—I had straightened the matter out. I told him I wanted Peggy's salary reverted to me at once, and he was to change her hotel reservations to double and I would pay the bill [with Peggy's money]. He said he could not change this— it was booked all through the tour for 12 weeks. I said very well, I would send him the amount but he was to revert me her salary. I advised him I had borrowed money to come east and promised a weekly payment on the loan and also gave my word to the Hotel Association I would make a weekly payment. He said okay and hung up. Two days later, he had still not cleared her salary to me, so I called him again and he refused to talk to me.

Before leaving Chicago, I consulted the law firm of Charles Short…regarding Dibs and our salary check. Mr. Short called the Dibs Agency, saying they should change this with the producer in each locale. He was informed Dibs could not legally do this unless I had given him a power of attorney. I told him on an occasion I had given him a power of attorney, which was for one

Having drinks with Alan Young in Chicago. (From the collection of Jeff Howard)

matter and only good for 48 hours, which was an occasion when Peggy and I were out of town and a picture was pending. On our return, this was void. Irrespective of this, Mr. Short drew a revocation of power of attorney and instructions to Mr. Dibs [that] as of that day all negotiations were null and void and any and all monies were to be deposited to the account at Citizens National Bank. This was mailed registered and I have a copy of same. This completed, Mr. Short thought I was secure and would have no further trouble. On the very strength of this, he cashed my personal check for $500.00 and I left Chicago for the next run of *Peg O' My Heart*. This was to Providence, RI. Incidentally, this revocation was mailed in June of 1949.

Closing in Providence on a Sunday, we are advised all checks would be forwarded to Baltimore, our next jump. Here I learned Peggy's checks had again gone to the coast, but I was not concerned as Mr. Dibs had been given instructions what to do. A week later, on arriving in New York, the Hotel Association jumped me, saying I had not kept my word. I could not register anywhere without paying in advance. Here, I also had a letter from Mr. Short saying Mr. Dibs had ignored his orders.

I was in a state of panic. I frantically called Mr. Dibs and told him I had to have some money and for him to at least send us Peggy's salary checks. He said no, not unless I signed her Excello contract. Peggy's expenses were provided for. I should come on home and, if I had no money, he would send me a ticket. The Hotel Association was breathing down my neck and threatening to have me arrested if I didn't make the promised payments. Charlie Hoffritz, by this time, was mad. I had not kept my word with him to pay so much weekly. But neither party were aware [that] no funds had come to my hands. I didn't dare be seen with Peggy because I was afraid of the Hotel Association. I was getting by on what money I still had from Mr. Farrow and Short for the $500.00 check I had cashed, but I could pay no bills. The situation became so bad with the Hotel Association I was afraid.

Finally, I went into New York [City] from Syracuse and confronted the Leonard Dibs Agency, begging them for help. They advised me they could book an extra week on *Peg O' My Heart* at Watkins Glen, NY. This salary or booking would be separate from the tour she was on and Dibs would not have any control, and this salary would be paid to us in Watkins Glenn at the close of the show. This was some relief, and I went to the Hotel Association and told them I would make a substantial payment when I got the check. This pacified them. I returned to Syracuse and stayed with friends until the show closed there.

I did not have funds to go with Peggy to Watkins Glenn, so I had to let her go on this jaunt alone.

It seems that Virginia's presence on the tour wasn't that helpful anyway since she was spending very little time with Peggy.

But by this time we were acquainted with the company, and I had asked an older woman to look after her. The understanding was Peggy would meet me in New York when the show closed. She would have been paid and brought me the money, and we would return to the coast together, but I would first pay the Hotel Association.

I met every train coming into New York from the Glenn one

whole night and no Peggy. I called her hotel at the Glenn and was advised she checked out before curtain time and was leaving for the airport from the theater. I called the theater and could get no information—only [that] she had left town and some friends had taken her to the airport. Checking on who the friends were, I called them. They said Peggy had left suddenly by plane for Chicago to do a television program. Her business manager had called her. I called Mr. Dibs; he would tell me nothing.

I borrowed some money from a friend and left for Chicago. I called everybody I ever knew and could not locate her. One report I got was she was in New York. My folks wired me money, and I went back to New York, only to find she was not there. Five full days had passed and I was frantic. I had no money, the Hotel Association were looking for me, and my child I couldn't find. I called Mr. Dibs again and he would tell me nothing, and at this point I told him I was going to the FBI.

Virginia was out of money and had no place to go. For three nights, she slept in the train station before being ordered to move on.

Peggy and troupe had flown across the country and back again twice before she saw her mother again. Virginia felt that she simply must rescue her child from the evil life that the industry was thrusting upon her. If she could persuade Peggy to go to college and get away from acting altogether, she thought, she might be able to accomplish that.

I called friends of mine in Washington, D.C., collect and asked them to meet me at the train. I told the conductor I had lost my wallet and had no money, and asked if I could ride to Washington and my fare would be paid on arrival. From Washington, I put through a call to Dibs and advised him I was not fooling; I was here to go to the FBI. Did he now want to tell me where my child was?

To my surprise, Mr. Garner got on the phone and advised me Peggy was all right, she was on the coast. He was there, had been for several days, and he was taking over. He said Dibs had called him and told him what a mess things were in, and it was my fault; and he was going to take things in hand. Dibs had not told him of the Excello contract. I told Mr. Garner to wire my

Peggy helping Betty Sullivan serve at a party.

fare to the coast. He said he didn't have it; he would have to get it
from Dibs.

I waited two days and my friends finally loaned me money
to return to the coast. I wired before my departure and advised Mr. Garner I was en route. He met me at the airport. In
the bar he picked up a friend, and we went into town. On the
way, Mr. Garner handed me a document. This was a notice
requesting me to resign as Peggy's legal guardian. This was
indeed a shock. I asked where Peggy was. Bill advised me he
had put her on a plane for New York about an hour before
mine came in. He said she had gone back to do a TV show
and would stay with the Ed Sullivans. Their daughter Betty
was Peggy's best friend, and I had had Betty in my home for
many months when she was going to school out here. I was
distressed not to have seen Peggy, but I felt she was in good
hands at the Sullivans'.

CHAPTER 12

Ed Sullivan was the powerful, but moody *New York Daily News* columnist and *Toast of the Town* host. Welcoming Peggy into their home in a two-room suite at the Delmonico Hotel provided a companion for their daughter, Betty.

As to resigning as Peggy's guardian, I flatly refused. I had done nothing to be removed. Our business affairs were in a mess, but only because of Dibs. The creditors were screaming, but this in time could have been worked out. I refused to resign, but agreed to let Mr. Garner become a co-guardian. This, he did not like.

My [Peggy's] home was leased. The apartment we had had been broken up and here I was, no money and my hands tied. Bill was giving me $5.00 a day and I was staying in third-rate hotels. This went on for two weeks. Dibs would not talk to me. Mr. Garner kept insisting I should agree to resigning from the guardianship—I would be relieved of the burden of the creditors hounding me. They would have to haunt him. This change would be temporary and, when things were cleared up, it would revert back to me. I told Bill he was not a resident of California and rarely ever here, [so] how could he act as guardian? He said temporarily he could. On this basis I said all right, but I was certainly going to tell the judge the reason for this. And I signed the notice of resignation. I was never served a notice of hearing and was not aware the date had been set. After I signed this, Mr. Garner provided me with a lovely Beverly Hills apartment.

Four days later and to my surprise came a headline story in the papers: Starlet's mother asked to resign guardianship of minor.

According to the *L. A. Times*, a petition was filed in September 1949, in Peggy's name, asking that her father replace her mother as her guardian. It said that she had already left Virginia's house in Las Vegas to live with her dad. This petition was filed through Bill Garner's attorney, H. Gregory Brilliant, and dealt with guardianship of the person only, not Peggy's assets, which totaled $36,095.08.

The story was heartbreaking and fantastic, stating my daughter and I had quarreled, she had accused me of extravagance, she had left the scene of her mansion, etc. This was all lies—Peggy and I never had the first word.

The hearing took place on October 5, and Superior Judge Newcomb Condee presided. The *L. A. Times* reported that it was stated at this hearing that Virginia and Peggy had quarreled over finances, and that Peggy complained about her mother's extravagant lifestyle. It was also stated that Virginia had no objections to the change of guardianship and her signed resignation was submitted to the Court by attorney Brilliant. He asked that father and daughter be allowed to live together at Peggy's S. Bentley Avenue house in Westwood. The court agreed and Bill Garner would now be Peggy's lawful guardian.

Neither Peggy nor I were at this hearing. She was in New York. I called Mr. Garner at his hotel and told him to meet me at Dibs. This was going to be retracted. It had to be. This was not good for Peggy. Bill and Dibs both denied issuing the story. I called Peggy in New York. She made no request for me to resign. The next day, I checked with the judge. He did not know where the story came from. I called Mr. Bishop, who had been our lawyer. He was not available.

A month later, Bill was again in court, objecting to the sale of Peggy's house for a mere $19,500 to furniture sales agent Leo Selditch and his wife, which had been proposed by Citizens National Trust & Savings Bank. $11,881.93 was still owed on it, and Bill felt it was worth a lot more than the price they would be paying. The judge suggested that Bill take over guardianship of Peggy's property, and decided to delay the hearing for a week while Bill discussed this with bank officials. Neither Peggy nor Virginia was there, nor at the hearing a week later in which the bank agreed to resign guardianship and Bill pledged, if he was given guardianship of Peggy's property, to make payments from his own pocket in order to save Peggy's house from forced sale. On December 7, Bill was appointed guardian of Peggy's estate by Judge Condee.

Less than a week later came another story on the front page. "Bank asked to resign as guardianship of starlet's estate"—Father takes over. This was beyond my understanding. I had no idea of any such plan. I again called Mr. Bishop. He was infuriated, blaming me, and would not talk to me. I, in return, was blaming him. Later to learn Mr. Garner had used another attorney, a man I had never heard of and a friend of Dibs. Why the bank was asked to resign was a mystery to me. Mr. Garner had only told me he had done it to save Peggy's money. He could figure her taxes and handle her investments. I was now without any jurisdiction, having been removed as her guardian.

Soon after the guardianship of the bank was changed to Mr. Garner, he had to leave California and return to Portland, Oregon, where he lived.

While Peggy and I had been in the east on tour, Mr. Dibs did not make the payments to the mortgage company on our furniture. As a result, the furniture was picked up, and the tenants who had paid the six months rent in advance had to vacate the empty house. This resulted in a suit against Peggy, which cost her $1,800.00, plus attorney fees and unfavorable publicity, again blaming me.

Peggy was still in New York and had been offered a New York stage play. She had written about it, and I said no, she was too young for Broadway, still only 17 years old. She was to return and go to college. This would give her something she would have all her life. She finally called about this play and begged to do it. I still rejected it and said she must return to California.

When she returned, her father was still here and she brought the script with her. The play was to be directed by Elia Kazan, the same director who had guided her to the Academy Award in *A Tree Grows in Brooklyn*. Her father said let her do the play. I insisted she go to college. Peggy wanted to do the play. This was compromised; it was agreed she would do the play. I was to return to New York with her. If the play was not a success, she was to return and enter college. This order, I demanded to be made an order of the court, and it was and is on record today. In spite of this, I had told her father, once she hit Broadway, she would never return to school. We called New York and advised them she would accept the play. In doing so, we were advised she had to be in New York two days later. I couldn't possibly leave that quick. There was so much to be straightened around.

Ed Sullivan called me and said she would be fine and was welcome to stay with them. This would be like trading daughters. (I have had their daughter several months.) It was understood Peggy would go on and I would be in New York in time for the opening. Peggy left and her father then returned to Portland. I was alone in Beverly Hills. This was October 1949.

Soon after returning to New York, Peggy appeared on Sullivan's *Toast of the Town* show. This took place on October 23. She also posed with Bob Stack beside his pool for a photo spread that appeared in the November issue of *Filmland* magazine. They were shown going through exercise routines together, with Stack serving as her trainer. Since Peggy seems never to have had an unfit day in her life, this was apparently done merely for publicity purposes. Keeping her in the public eye was crucial to her career.

Mr. Garner was working with Mr. Dibs, but to what extent I did not know. But whenever I needed information, I had to call Dibs. When it was time for me to go to New York, he told me not to go. This would be wasting money. Peggy was in good hands and she had no expenses. His next excuse was the play may flop and then it would be coming back to California, so it was foolish.

Xmas, I was alone.

CHAPTER 13

Peggy would make her debut on the Broadway stage in the play titled *The Man*. During the pre-Broadway performances at the Nixon Theater in Pennsylvania, she was interviewed at the Pittsburgher Hotel by *Pittsburgh Post-Gazette* reporter James W. Ross. Peggy related to him that she was now in an awkward stage.

"Ha! Every woman twice her age should be so awkward!" he responded.

What she meant was that, three weeks shy of her eighteenth birthday, she was too old for children's roles and too young to be the leading lady. "I'd really like to do a musical," she said, "but I don't look like Elizabeth Taylor, so that's out."

"Yes, she sings. And yes, she doesn't look like Elizabeth Taylor," Ross wrote. "But in her own way, Peggy did all right by the fluffy yellow sweater she wore. The little girl parts are definitely gone for good."

Besides her candor, reporters noticed something else unusual about Peggy—she chewed her fingernails. She was hoping to have that habit broken once the show got to Broadway, but she was too nervous about the play to quit right away.

Opening night for *The Man* was on January 19, 1950, at the Fulton Theatre. Peggy gave ninety-two performances during the play's run. Co-starring with her were Dorothy Gish, Don Hanmer, Robert Emhardt, Richard Boone, Frank McNellis, and Josh White, Jr. Peggy told Ross, "Miss Gish is so nice to work with—I play her niece, sort of comedy relief—well—it's just different." (Her friend, Barbara Whiting, would play Peggy's role in the movie version, *Beware, My Lovely* in 1952.)

> The play opened. Nothing spectacular. It closed in March. I thought sure Peggy would return. This had been the agreement.
> Mr. Sullivan called me again and asked that she be permitted to stay a while longer. It would do her good and she could be doing television. My health was so broken and I had no clothes, my luggage being held at the Hotel Association. I simply couldn't work. I was depending on Mr. Garner and my family for support—Mr. Garner's portion allotted to me through Mr. Dibs.

After *The Man* closed, Peggy did some television work in New York. She appeared in *Tele-Theatre's* "Once to Every Boy" and "Call It a Day," then, in March of 1950, Peggy and Bill Williams appeared on a television show together. The following month, she helped him publicize the opening of a television store in the Bronx.

According to the article "Peggy Co-Ed," in the April 1950 issue of *Screen Stars*, Peggy had begun attending the University of Southern California and was majoring in psychology and dramatics. This, she felt, would serve her well in her career—dramatics for the obvious reason, and psychology to enable her to thoroughly understand her characters. It appears that this photo spread had been taken much earlier with the thought that, when this issue of the magazine was released, Peggy would indeed be in college. In actuality, though, she was still living in New York when it came out. USC's verification department reports that there's a card on file with only Peggy's name—but no dates or courses listed. Apparently, she applied to the college, but did not actually attend because she was too busy working.

> Finally in May, I could stand it no longer. I said if Peggy was to remain in New York and that was what she wanted, her place was with her mother, where she would have proper supervision and I would know what she was doing. Mr. Dibs told me she was in good hands.
> I was aware of Mrs. Sullivan being away on various occasions and this left Peggy alone in the apartment with Ed. This I did not approve of and feared for Peggy's well being. I called Mr. Garner and told him he was the guardian now and respon-

sible. Either he send me to New York or return Peggy, or I was going to Judge Scott and have her returned by court order. He wired me money to go. I called Mr. Dibs and told him I needed some clothes, which Mr. Garner had told me to do. Dibs told me I had a checking account. I bought a suit and a hat, which totaled $117.21, and gave a check in this amount and one for a pair of shoes. That night before leaving, I called Peggy at Sullivan's and told her I was leaving for New York the next day. I also called Dibs and told him what clothes I purchased and he should be sure there was money to cover the checks.

When I arrived in New York, I called Peggy at Sullivan's. I was told she had gone to the Poconos. This completely floored me. She knew I was coming. I had not seen her for six months, and I was at a loss to understand. I heard this same story for 10 straight days. During this interim, I had called Dibs and her father, and I could get no information. On Mother's Day, May 18th, I called my mother in Ohio to wish her a Happy Day and [told her] how alone I felt with Peggy being up in the Poconos in Pennsylvania. My mother said she was not there; she was in Florida. This was really a shock. I again called Sullivan and was told she was in the Poconos. Half an hour later, I had the bell captain at the Plaza call and ask for Peggy, and he was advised she was in Florida. Then I called Sullivan and asked him what the idea was. He turned the phone over to Carmen, his secretary. Carmen claimed he knew nothing and Ed had just stepped out. I called Dibs in California and Mr. Garner in Portland; they would tell me nothing. I tried calling various hotels in Florida and can produce today the phone bill for all these calls. Over this bill, I had to leave my luggage I had come to New York with because I couldn't pay the bill. This also I can prove.

Desperate, panicky and in despair over my child, I went to Sherman Billingsly at the Stork Club, whom I know was a close friend of Walter Winchell. I knew Winchell was in Florida, and if Peggy was there he could find her. Mr. Billingsley had a daughter Peggy's age and he knew my concern. He told me to return in half an hour or he would call me. He did and had talked to Winchell. Peggy was in Florida at Kitty Davis Restaurant. I called Sullivan and informed him I was going after Peggy. I left that night. I found where she had been staying—at Sydney Miller's. But she had left that morning and was cruising in the Bahamas. I couldn't find her on the ocean, so I returned to New York.

Calling Sullivan, I gave him 24 hours to have Peggy in New York or I was going to the police. The next afternoon, Peggy knocked on the door of my hotel room. I never saw a girl look so pitiful. My heart ached for her. I asked her what she was doing in Florida and why had she left when she knew I was coming to NY and why Ed Sullivan had lied to me. All she could do was cry. I told her we were going to see Ed. She said Ed couldn't see me until in the morning. Peggy said she would come and get me and bring me some hose and a clean blouse. The only clothes I had were on my back.

Peggy's tears could well have been due to compassion for her mother. The poor woman had been all over creation looking for her, apparently without a change of clothing, and probably looked quite bedraggled.

The next morning, we walked into Sullivan's. Ed was there alone. I was told to get out of town, I wasn't needed, my child was happy there with him and I was to leave her alone. If I attempted to take her away, he would call the police. He told me I was no good, no one had any use for me and the farther away I stayed the better it would be. He told me he would have the Hotel Association get me. And besides that, there was a warrant for my arrest on a check in California. I told him I was not afraid of the Hotel Association. I would go and talk to them and if I could only pay them 5 cents a week, I was sure they would work with me, if they knew I was in good faith. The warrant I knew nothing about, but I would call Dibs or Mr. Garner, and I was not afraid.

Since Virginia had recently stayed at the Plaza, her earlier hotel bills must have been paid, so it might have been all the phone calls she made there that got her in hot water again.

Sullivan then asked me how much money I had, and I told him very little. He put $20.00 in my shoulder bag and said "This will get you to Ohio where your family are. Maybe they want you." Then he said "Or I will put you on a plane and make sure you don't get off until you get to California." I told him he must be crazy or on dope to talk in such a manner. I said if New York is what Peggy wanted, all well and good, but she would be with her mother. I would go to work, but she would have my supervision. Then I told him I would go immediately to the Hotel Association if that was what concerned him. But I was going nowhere. I came to New York and to be with my child. Ed was very perturbed and said he would talk to the Hotel Association for me, and I should call him the next morning.

Through all of this, Peggy sat sobbing.

Virginia interpreted Peggy's tears to mean that she was being mistreated here and needed to be rescued. In reality, they seem to have meant that she was terribly afraid that her mother would take her away from the Sullivans. Here is how Peggy's feelings were expressed in an interview she had later with Dick Moore for his book *Twinkle, Twinkle, Little Star*: "Peggy spent her happiest years with Ed Sullivan and his wife and daughter. At last she had a family [that included, very importantly, a father figure], emotional support, and the courage to confront her mother for the first time, and to tell her father 'all the things that had been going on for years.'" Sullivan was apparently aware of these feelings of Peggy's and was bound and determined not to let Virginia whisk her away, ruining her happiness.

I left the apartment completely shattered. I went to a friend in Wall Street, a highly-respected person, married and has four children. Related the whole situation, and he said he wanted to talk to Peggy. We called her at Sullivan's, and she met us in the lobby of the Clinton Hotel where I was staying. Peggy and I both had cried so much we looked terrible, so I suggested we go up to my room. I failed to mention when I approached my friend in Wall Street, I was so disturbed and so upset I could hardly talk. He got me a shot of whiskey to quiet me.

When we got in my room, my friend asked Peggy if she could account for Mr. Sullivan talking to her mother the way he did. Peggy started to cry and said she couldn't take anymore. I raised my voice then and said what did she think about her mother? What did she think *she* could take? My friend said we were both upset, we should get some rest and he would talk to us the next morning. He left the hotel with Peggy and dropped her off at the Delmonico where the Sullivans lived.

The next morning, I called Ed for his report on what the Hotel Association said. Mr. Sullivan screamed at me, saying "You no-good bum! You had a man in your room in the presence of your daughter, drunk!"

[So that explains why Peggy cried instead of explaining further that Sullivan had been defending her when she had had all she could take from her mother. Then it was made worse when the inebriated man took Peggy from Virginia's hotel room back to the Sullivans' hotel. She had obviously shared her dismay with Sullivan, hoping he would again intercede.]

I was numb, and asked him if he had lost his mind. He told me to leave my daughter alone and to get out of town or what he would do—then again threatened to break my skull if I talked. This was May of 1950.

I wrote Mr. Garner in detail about this and he never made any comment.

CHAPTER 14

I stayed in New York and worked at any job I could get—did some laundry work, waited tables, jerked soda, etc. I had only the clothes on my back, a white blouse and a navy suit. Every night I washed the blouse.

I called Peggy about once a week, and she would meet me in some public place, and we talked a few minutes. Peggy always had to go right away and acted as though someone was watching her and she was afraid. I lived in fear of Ed Sullivan and was careful not to let Peggy know where I was staying. In eight months in New York, I moved 46 different times to hotels, spending a few days at a time.

Knowing where show and TV people frequented, I would loiter in hopes of seeing Peggy. During these months, I began to hear very disparaging remarks about my daughter and Ed. I would write her father and he ignored me, resulting in I listened to gossip. On one occasion, when I found pills on Peggy, I became frantic and called her father to come to New York the next week. The night he came in, he, Peggy and I had dinner. We had no chance to talk about anything. At the table, she announced she was going to Florida that night. I asked her why and who with. She would say nothing. I said she couldn't go. Her father said it would be good for her, she was tired. Peggy left the table, came back later, and flashed a ticket to Florida. And she left that night. I argued with her father until I was blue in the face. Where was his mind? This 18-year-old girl flitting to all parts of the country. He was guardian and responsible. My hands were tied.

I asked Mr. Garner if he was going to see Sullivan or if Sullivan had called him. He said no and why should he see Sullivan? I gave him plenty of reasons and told him to get Peggy out of that apartment. Mr. Garner and I continued to quarrel and he left in a huff for Portland. Next, in desperation, I sent for my folks in Ohio. Both Mother and Dad came and they tried to help me with Peggy. Peggy would not talk to any of us more than a few minutes at a time. They gave up and went home. We knew there was a mystery, but what we have never been able to learn ... I could take no more and decided to head west. Possibly Judge Scott could help me from this end.

I stopped in Ohio to visit my folks. They were so willing to help me. While here, I dreamed up a way to get Peggy out of New York. If it would only work. Columbus was close by and Ohio State College was there. This team had played the Rose Bowl in 1940 and, after the game we had the team at our home in Beverly Hills. Peggy was their mascot and dearly loved. This year, they were playing in the Orange Bowl. Maybe I could persuade the college to invite Peggy to Miami as their mascot. Xmas was only a week away. I went to Columbus, made the deal, Peggy's agents were wired. They offered her all expenses and $1,000.00 for the appearance. The wire came back [saying] she would accept. I worked all week in Columbus, making plans.

Here, I went to Lazarus store and told them about the program. Peggy was not with me, but I would join her in Florida. They selected a full wardrobe of what she might need and a few things for me. I gave them a check for $750.00 with the understanding this would be held until it was decided what we would keep and what would be returned. A second check or payment would be supplemented. And I cashed a check which also was to be held until my return. However, they were written on my own bank in Los Angeles. I left my hotel for the airport. Before departure, I called Peggy at Sullivan's. Mrs. Sullivan talked to me. Peggy was not home. I advised her I was leaving for Florida and would meet Peggy there New Year's Day. [Virginia had just sabotaged her own scheme.]

Peggy did not show up. Once again, my heart was broken.

Peggy loved football and was probably delighted to accept the honor until she found out it wasn't a true invitation but, rather, had been arranged by her mother in a manipulative move. Peggy was now obviously avoiding Virginia, but Virginia refused to see it.

> **I returned the clothes to Columbus and advised them to hold the checks. Just as soon as I could get to California, they would be taken care of. Then I wrote to Mr. Garner to take care of same.**

Producers and press agents were urging Peggy to shorten her name, but she steadfastly held on to the three-parter that had been so much a part of her life. Cornelia Otis Skinner could, she reasoned, so why couldn't she? Good point!

Although Peggy's heart was in Hollywood and she had recently appeared in the film *Teresa*, she was now working mostly on stage and in live television in New York. She was cast next in *The Royal Family*, as Gwen, at the New York Center. Peggy received third billing in the program, under Ruth Hussey and Ethel Griffies. The play ran for only sixteen performances, however.

In the book *Secrets of the Stars*, by Denis Myers, notes:

> **Talking of beauty—and beauty aids—you might look twice at Peggy Ann Garner, an appealing blonde who played opposite Pier Angeli in *Teresa*. For eight years Peggy Ann was probably the only actress who never wore make-up on the screen. That was when she was a juvenile "promise." Then she played a fifteen-year-old bobbysoxer in *Home Sweet Homicide*. For the first time she was allowed to use lipstick. But only on the screen. Mrs. Garner, senior, is not so strict now.**

With this mention in the book is an accompanying photo of a scene from *Teresa* in which Peggy and John Ericson, who played siblings in the film, are embracing while looking at each other with love in their eyes. Peggy was indeed wearing lipstick and looked beautiful.

Back on the home front, Peggy's friend, Rosemary Clooney, was a regular on the show *Songs for Sale* and was rehearsing nearby, so Peggy dropped in to say hello. There, she met a delightful young man, Richard Hayes, Mercury

Records' hot new singer. He would soon have two hit records under his belt, "Too Young" and "Fast Freight." Brooklyn-born Richard, a handsome and congenial man only two years older than Peggy, was also a regular on this show. The two liked each other right away and began dating. After a while, the courtship turned quite serious and they began talking marriage.

Peggy studied for a short time at the Actor's Studio. It was quite prestigious to be a member of this respected organization, but their standards were extremely high and they took acting much too seriously for Peggy's taste. Lee Strasberg, the founder of the Studio, looked down on film and television work as inferior. One of his pet phrases was "Movies are not art." To him, the stage was the only legitimate form of acting. For the first time, Peggy's confidence in her acting ability was shaken and she wasn't receiving the approval she needed.

"One thing I'll never do, and this is a particular peeve of mine, is go to any drama school to improve myself," she told the *Newark Sunday News* a few years later. "So many young actors are doing it these days, and it's bad because talent and individuality can be stifled by studied attention to technique and reflexes. These schools can sometimes mold fine technicians out of untalented people, but they can do so much damage to the genuinely creative artist."

Peggy left the Studio.

Meanwhile, Virginia was stranded in Florida with the Rose Bowl, in a trap of her own making.

> Here I was in Miami—stumped, broke, defeated in every way. My mind wandered seriously on the side of suicide. This, I decided, was a sign of failure. My parents wired me money. I called Peggy. Her only excuse was she couldn't make it. I told her I would spend a few days here and go on to the coast. I did some snooping in Miami Beach and located a young girl who was a friend of Betty Sullivan and Peggy, whom I had met in New York. I called and we had lunch. I asked her if she knew who Peggy had been with when she was in Miami in April and May. She said she didn't know; she saw very little of her. This girl did tell me Peggy had told her if any woman ever asked her anything, don't give her any information. It will be a relative who is trying to cause her some trouble.
>
> This came as another jolt. I decided to try and see Walter Winchell. He lived down here. I made an appointment. As I

left my hotel, two men approached me and asked where I was going. They advised me I'd better not try to see Winchell. They advised me to leave town that night.

In Dallas, we had friends that were very close to Margaret Truman. Margaret was friendly with Peggy. I thought maybe through this, they could help. To Dallas I went. Related my tale of woe to the Harpers. They knew Peggy so well Mr. Harper called Peggy and begged her to come to Dallas and visit on their ranch. Mr. Harper told Peggy I was there. [Big mistake!] Peggy in return told Mr. Harper I wanted to cause her trouble. He called Mr. Garner. Bill said Peggy was fine and pay no attention to gossip.

Meanwhile, Peggy and her co-stars had opened in the play entitled *The Royal Family* on January 10, 1951. It ran for sixteen performances, then closed.

The timing was perfect.

She was now free to tackle a bigger project for ABC-TV—a television series of her own called *Two Girls Named Smith*. It premiered on January 20, 1951, and aired on Saturdays at noon. Co-starring as the other girl named Smith was another girl named Peggy—Broadway actress Peggy French. Produced by Richard Lewis and directed by Charles S. Dubin, this was a thirty-minute situation comedy that was sponsored by the makers of Bab-O and Glim. Peggy Ann played Babs Smith, an aspiring model who had moved to Manhattan from Omaha. Her roommate, Fran Smith, was her cousin, an aspiring artist/fashion designer. They would get into one delightful and daffy adventure after another. For the noon broadcast, actors had to be on the set by 7:30 a.m. They were the fortunate ones. The crew had already been there several hours by that time.

I left Harpers and checked into a hotel. I called Mr. Garner for money to get me to California. He refused to send it, saying he would send me a ticket to Portland. There was nothing for me in Portland, but I was sure Judge Scott could help me in California. I had heard Mr. Garner had converted Peggy's insurance to cash and many other things, and I wanted to see the court records. I knew I could find out a great deal. Under law, he should have given an accounting to the court for her earnings; something had to show. I knew he was working with Dibs, but

The stars of *Two Girls Named Smith*, Peggy French and Peggy Ann Garner.

how or under what set-up, I did not know. Peggy had done two pictures, but where the money was, I did not know. She claimed she had no money.

Here in Dallas, I decided to go to the police department and tell them about the warrant for me in California and ask to be held for extradition. The Captain of Police laughed at me when he could find no record of a warrant. He told me to get going. So I thought if I got arrested, they would have to hold me. To do this, I called a store, ordered a nightgown and ordered it charged to a fictitious name and delivered to me at my hotel.

On January 30, 1951, Virginia, going by the name Kathryn Whitaker, was arrested in Ft. Worth, Texas. The charges were the theft of more than fifty dollars and fraudulent use of a charge account. On February 15, she was also charged with theft under fifty dollars—cashing a worthless twenty-five-dollar check at the LAX bar where, the bartender said, she was a regular customer. She was sentenced to thirty days in the county jail and fined $23.50 costs.

According to an article in the *Herald Express*, she also had a bad-check warrant out for her in Shreveport, Louisiana.

> From here, I wired [the sheriff] to extradite me on the warrant they had. I wired Mrs. Terry and Judge Scott to push this.
>
> Nothing came through. I have copies of these wires. Three weeks later, it was announced I was in jail in Dallas over the networks. Then I wrote Peggy and Mr. Sullivan, saying this would return me to California and I would be tried on the warrant there. Here, I would relate what happened from the beginning. The next I knew, a reporter from the *New York News* came to see me at the jail. I refused to see him.

While Virginia was serving her time in a Texas jail, she missed a very important day in her daughter's life.

CHAPTER 15

On February 22, 1951, Peggy became Mrs. Richard H. Hayes. This was the first marriage for them both and it was a grand affair, staged in the Banquet Room of the Delmonico Hotel on Park Avenue in New York and hosted by Ed Sullivan, who gave the bride away. Barbara Whiting was her maid of honor, Rosemary Clooney and Jackie Sherman her bridesmaids for this double-ring ceremony. Fifty guests attended, but neither of Peggy's parents were there. Virginia was, of course, detained in Texas, but what about Peggy's father?

Neither had been invited.

"She had no desire to have her mother there," says Richard. "She had no desire, I assume, to have her father there." It would soon become apparent to Richard how distressed Peggy was by her mother and how seldom her father was around.

Ed and Sylvia Sullivan signed the marriage certificate as witnesses, while Peggy's new mother-in-law happily told reporters, "We were crazy about Peggy the first time Dick brought her home. We all love her and want to be a real family to her."

Because of their heavy television schedule—he in NBC's *Broadway Open House* and she in *Two Girls Named Smith*—the newlyweds were not able to take time off for a honeymoon. Instead, they settled into their own two-room apartment at the Mayflower Hotel overlooking Central Park. It was already furnished, but they hoped to replace some pieces with furniture of their own someday. The bell that had been atop their wedding cake served as a sentimental centerpiece for their living room table. Maid service was theirs and, whenever they needed anything, all they had to do was call out for it. They usually had their meals in restaurants.

Peggy's big day. Ed Sullivan walks the beaming bride down the aisle and hosts the reception. (From the collection of Connie Stratton)

Peggy put her love for California out of her mind. She would not go back there unless Hollywood called Richard, too. Being with him was her top priority now.

Once she learned of their marriage, Virginia was heartsick over the whole situation. This union wasn't what it seemed, she told people. She was sure that the studio moguls or perhaps Ed Sullivan had coerced Peggy and Richard into it so Virginia would no longer have any authority over her daughter. (Once married, Peggy was legally considered an adult.) Or perhaps it was forced for publicity purposes.

"No," Richard said, "that never happened." The marriage had been

Peggy and Richard's idea, no one else's. Virginia was very much out of touch with what was going on in Peggy's life and was putting ominous meanings to the little that she saw.

The Los Angeles Times reported in March that Virginia was accused of swindling money from an orphan. While in Waukegan the previous summer to be with Peggy, who was appearing in summer stock in Wheeling, it seems Virginia made a promise to nineteen-year-old Barbara Ann Kiran to get her into the movies if she would give her $500. Barbara scrounged up $450, Virginia took it, and Barbara never heard from her again. It was a confidence game, they said, and State Attorney Robert C.

"I now pronounce you man and wife." Rosemary Clooney looks on.
(From the collection of Connie Stratton)

Sharing a happy moment at the reception with Sylvia Sullivan.
(From the collection of Connie Stratton)

Nelson ordered them to issue a warrant for her arrest. Could this be one of the "friends" from whom Virginia had "borrowed" money?

> Waiting almost two months to hear from Los Angeles and nothing happening, I was pretty down. Then from Ohio came a hold. This was on the two checks I left at Lazarus, when I tried to get Peggy to Florida. When they learned I was in jail, they turned these checks in to the DA. From Dallas, I was extradited to Ohio. California would not come and get me.
>
> I was satisfied returning to Ohio because my folks were close by and would be able to help me. When Judge Harter

got the facts, he said it would be unjust to try me on these checks. In the first place, they had never been sent to the bank; secondly, in view of the circumstances related along with what he learned had taken place in Columbus.

My folks had retained counsel for me in Columbus, and this counsel contacted Mr. Garner for information. Mr. Garner wrote this lawyer [that] I was neurotic and he wanted me committed to a state hospital.

Virginia had been held in custody in Ohio from April through June 1951, then was released on a $2,500 bond and told to return to California and get her affairs in order.

Posing with her surrogate parents, Ed and Sylvia Sullivan, and new hubby Richard. (From the collection of Connie Stratton)

Soon after this, Virginia and Peggy were sued by Carl B. Bickel for furniture they had bought and not finished paying for. Of the original $8,000 charges, there was still $4,088 owing. Peggy and Virginia did not appear at this proceeding, but were represented by Bill Garner. He told the Court that Peggy had neither participated in that purchase nor benefited from the furniture, so it didn't seem fair that she would be included in this lawsuit. Superior Judge Ingall W. Bull agreed and ruled that Peggy was not to be held responsible for her mother's furniture bills.

En route from Columbus to California, I stopped in Idaho to see Mr. Garner and I begged him to help me get Peggy out of New York. The girl had had no home, no supervision since the day he took over as the guardian. He would do nothing. So I left and returned to California.

On court record, I found where Mr. Garner had gotten in excess of $5,000.00 on one occasion, claiming he had advanced such a sum to further his child's career...On another occasion, he was allotted in excess of $1,000.00 for services acting as her guardian. Later I learned Mr. Garner's motive for me to resign as guardian was simply to give him access to her estate. Mr. Garner needed some money to work with Dibs. If he had control of the house, he could borrow his needed funds. This he did in the amount of $4,000.00. Later he sold the house, giving no account to the court of Peggy's funds when she reached her majority.

Peggy consistently maintained she had no money. She had worked a great deal and she should have been well fixed. My suspicion was when Dibs could not get me to sign his contract and I had terminated his service by registered mail, he was in trouble someplace and he had to call Mr. Garner when he found I had put him out. Replacing Mr. Garner reestablished Dibs in Peggy's affairs. I believe her funds had been transferred to New York and were dumped into some shady corporation...Peggy was a minor when this took place, and I stood legally as her guardian, but I was given no knowledge or notice of this.

Peggy has been led to believe her mother squandered her money. And this was all I was trying to prove and put before the authorities so it could be investigated.

CHAPTER 16

Life in Manhattan was a stimulating, exciting experience for Peggy and Richard. Restaurants and theaters were easily accessible. This glittering couple could often be seen at parties and around town, and their careers were going quite well. Nina Foch, who was a regular on *Two Girls Named Smith*, would sometimes see Peggy again at these parties. "She was very nice and sweet," she said. Peggy had many illustrious friends who would visit them at home—Roddy McDowall, Barbara Whiting, and Pier Angeli, to name a few. She would frequently receive calls from her friend Betty Sullivan, as well. Life was so good.

Peggy had a personal goal now. "I just want to be with Dick. I really don't care about my career because I'm so anxious to have a family," she told reporters. Her greatest ambition was to be a good wife and mother.

There *was* a third member of the family now. Richard and Peggy had a little cocker spaniel puppy and named her Miss McCocoa.

Even though Peggy was busy with *Two Girls Named Smith*, she managed to squeeze in an appearance with hubby Richard on *The Kate Smith Hour* on March 22. Her life was very full and very happy.

The couple felt that they needed to get a place of their own. Their dear friend Rosemary Clooney lived in an apartment a few blocks from them on Fifty-Seventh Street, so they moved there. Proudly displayed on the shelf of their new home was Peggy's Oscar.

The decision makers of the popular *Two Girls Named Smith* wanted her character, Babs, to have a boyfriend. Could Richard, her real-life husband, play the part?

"I had never done any acting," he recalls. "I said 'I don't know.'"

131

After mulling it over, he decided "Why not? Let me take a stab at it," and was promptly cast in the part.

The show was getting good viewership, being in the top five of the weekend daytime shows. Its distribution was one of the highest for a network show in this era, with fifty-three cities carrying it.

Richard would frequently go on singing tours when he wasn't needed on the series. This posed a problem. Peggy needed her man to be present in her life on a daily basis, as her father had not been. She would rather go with Richard on his tours than continue on the show, so she quit the series in September. Her replacement was Marcia Henderson. In October, the series was cancelled. The final show was broadcast on October 13, 1951. Peggy didn't care. She was with Richard more now and, best of all, she was going to be a mother in May. She was ecstatic.

Later that month, Richard had nightclub engagements in Canton and Cleveland. Peggy accompanied her husband to Ohio. "She used to come with me to these things," Richard said.

Peggy couldn't pass up this opportunity to go visit her relatives in Canton and Akron and introduce them to her handsome new hubby. The

Peggy quit her hit TV series to go with Richard on tour.
(From the collection of Connie Stratton)

It's good to be with the relatives again. Back: Cameron Brogden, Peggy and
Cameron Brogden Jr. Front: Carol Brogden and Joy Craig.
(From the collection of Connie Stratton)

October 26, 1951 edition of *The Canton Repository* shows a beaming Peggy
and Richard, looking together at an album. "There's no dearth of childhood pictures in this photograph album," says the caption. "Peggy Ann
Garner shows husband Richard Hayes some of the many pictures of herself collected by one of her most ardent admirers, her grandmother. Mrs.
Shields Craig of 1619 Fulton Rd. NW possesses four or five such albums,
most of them filled with shots of Peggy taken during periods of her movie,
stage and television career." Now that their work with *Two Girls Named
Smith* was over, Peggy told the reporter, "Our big ambition now is to have
a Mr. and Mrs. television show."

Richard added "Something with music in it. You may not know it,
but Peggy can sing too."

"Yes, I'd probably end up singing and you'd be acting," Peggy joked.

From that day (Friday) through Sunday, Richard made appearances
at the Casablanca nightclub. Then it was on to Cleveland. Peggy stayed
with relatives for a few days while he fulfilled that commitment.

Entertainers there were treated well and given a Nash car to drive while in the Cleveland area. Then Richard received disturbing news. "I get a call one night—I was at the club—that she miscarried. She was in the hospital." Not knowing whether Peggy was dead or alive, or any details about their lost baby, Richard got into the Nash and rushed from Cleveland to Canton. It was October 31, Halloween night. Not only was he in the dark about his wife, but he was also wondering why people in the various cities' village greens looked so pleased to see him pass by. "How did they know?" he wondered. It was later that he realized the Nash had his name painted on its side. The townsfolk were excited to see a familiar celebrity from television among them.

Once he arrived at Peggy's bedside in the hospital, he was relieved to find that she was all right.

It appears that Peggy was unaware that her mother was spending much of her time in jail these days. To her and Richard, Virginia seemed to disappear for periods of time without explanation, then pop into their lives again, usually in a quite unpleasant manner.

Three months after her release from the Columbus jail, Virginia was arrested in the lobby of a fashionable San Francisco hotel. Some exclusive peninsula shops had reported to police that she had paid for large quantities of ladies' clothing and accessories by check, then returned them for cash before the store owners realized the checks were no good. To do this, she had obtained three fictitious driver's licenses and used the aliases Mrs. Elizabeth D. Sanford, Nancy Kent Hanna, and Mrs. Winifred M. Kertz. The *L. A. Examiner* reported that "Mrs. Garner said it was all 'just a mixup' and she had believed the checks to be covered by deposits." Why couldn't the people in charge of Peggy's business get these things straight, she wondered, feeling that they should have made the money available to her. She was taken to Burlingame to be booked.

On December 5, the day her trial was to begin, Virginia changed her plea from "not guilty" to "guilty by reason of insanity" regarding nine charges of passing bad checks. Judge Scott then ordered her to be examined by two psychiatrists, and he set the date of December 18 for her trial, without a jury, on the insanity issue.

While in jail, Virginia arranged for the Wrap 'n Woof Shop to send material to her. She then made it into an elegant outfit for Peggy. Sheriff Whitmore's deputy obligingly mailed it to her daughter in New York for Christmas.

On January 29, 1952, Virginia's case was decided. She had been tested by two doctors and deemed sane, so she was found guilty of forgery and sentenced to one to five years at the California Institution for Women at Tehachapi. Because she was incarcerated here, she was unable to appear for her trial set for the previous arrest, and, consequently, her bond was revoked. All because of a crooked business manager, she said.

Virginia wrote to Los Angeles District Attorney Ernest Rolls, explaining her situation in general terms. She didn't want clemency, she assured him. She didn't want the earlier charge dropped. All she wanted was her day in court, and it must be in Los Angeles so that there would be media coverage as the evildoers would be hauled into court and finally held accountable for their actions. "Your office may find itself deeply interested in many of the ramifications that will unfold themselves," she assured him. "If you should deem it proper to return me to Los Angeles," she wrote, "may I suggest please, that it be as close to immediately as is feasible, because most of the principals involved in the case will be on the west coast within the next few weeks, and that it be done quietly in order not to alert any of the same people who might prefer not to appear and testify." Now, she thought, she'll be able to expose what she felt were the evil goings-on in the entertainment industry.

It wasn't action on Rolls' part but, rather, an earthquake in Tehachapi that was responsible for Virginia's change in location. But it didn't matter. She was now where she wanted to be—in Los Angeles.

Her happiness was short-lived, however, when she received a message from Superior Court Judge A. A. Scott that she might not have to stand trial after all. Virginia immediately wrote him a very lengthy letter, pleading for a hearing and stating the reasons why:

> **To dismiss this, Judge Scott, to me, would be a personal disaster of gigantic proportions. I come to you in all humility praying for help to guide my child's welfare. When I wrote you originally, I hoped to be able to confer with you personally. I still hope to, but now the imminence of our meeting depends upon factors beyond my control.**
>
> **There is much in this case history that will astound you Judge Scott. Were it not for the verifiable facts and my own sorrowful participation in them, I would find the situation fiction too melodramatic for my taste. If however...in Peggy's**

name…you will lend me your ears and your heart, I'll try to be coherent and as brief as I can.

A check written by me and dated April 1950, resulted in the hold against me which I signed in Miss Holzschuh's office, and which I hoped would return me to Los Angeles for trial—as close to immediately as possible. Please be assured, Judge Scott, that I am completely aware of the fact that a verdict of guilty could lengthen my present stay in the Institution. I neither expect nor ask for leniency from the Court nor Board of Trustees—but I beg for the opportunity of removing the bandages from the eyes of Justice by revealing the entire truth behind this bizarre mess.

This one check—and its background—is the key to as sordid a story as you have judged in your years as an administrator of justice. No less than five major transgressions could be placed before the court;

How a disreputable business manager wrote fraudulent contracts for the expressed purpose of evading honest income tax returns, relative to Peggy's income.

How this same business manager sent my daughter out of the state without my approval and against my wishes; doing so by refusing to issue checks for my transportation, for this purpose had her sign her earnings over to his New York lawyers, and withheld knowledge of the whereabouts of a minor child from her legal guardian in order to stall for time in which to form a holding company in New York which he could not get passed here (something forbidden by the California <u>Coogan Law</u>.)

How this chicanery and perjury and who conspired with Mr. Garner, who resides in Portland Oregon, and not in the state of California, to remove this minor child's mother as her legal guardian by defamation of character, basing his petition on lies and which resulted in a tragic false story that hit the press nationally. The latter, released so that the forementioned business manager could not be exposed by said mother. The child's father was in no way entitled to guardianship as the mother had been granted full custody by the court in 1939, and again in 1945, during their divorce action. The purpose of this was to later remove the Bank as guardian of the estate, so money could be borrowed against her home for capitol needed, which they did.

How the said business manager cashed and dispursed funds of this minor child, and further endorsed and disbursed funds of tax refund checks which her father, acting as guardian, had full knowledge of. He advised me accordingly, yet would do nothing to expose this character, because it put him in a light which he preferred not to have brought to the attention of the authorities.

How he arranged employment for her that was not approved, under the Coogan Law, by the courts, and put her to work.

This is a resume of five crimes perpetrated against my minor daughter, Peggy Ann, by the business manager. The web in which he has implicated himself, and several name personalities, and which is basically the reason for my being in the California Institution for Women today. This I might add, Judge Scott, only touches the rough spots of what has gone on behind the scenes which literally wrecked the lives of two people, my daughter and I, to say nothing of the heartache that goes with it.

Peggy Ann was only seventeen when this ugly confusion began and which has constantly continued. Even her marriage was constituted by their advice and for the sole purpose, that it would lend to their protection, as it constituted her being an adult. Therefore if any action should be brought, on this basis, it would have to be done by her personally, but with their deplorable method of contaminating her mind they felt safe that such action was not likely, however this said marriage is completely shattered and the picture changed.

If it is not unravelled thoroughly and honestly, I fear for Peggy's future welfare; for her mental equilibrium and for her spiritual well-being. You remember Peggy, Judge Scott, the sweet serenity that we love so dearly to associate with youth, her integrity of purpose and being, the shining Pixie goodness of America's Junior Miss. She doesn't radiate anymore Judge Scott—The glow's been turned off inside her, she's a terrified little girl, too frightened to speak even in her own defense, and I know of no one who can soothe her fears and thaw her terror into a feeling of safety except perhaps you Judge Scott. I can not help but feel and trust that you will agree with me on this fact—that it should be me as her Mother and not Peggy Ann to expose this entire situation. I base my opinion on two reasons;

> For Peggy personally or in part to relate these situations to Your Honor, or to the District Attorney, she could not avoid implicating her father and this imposition I feel would be unjust and place on her conscience a scar that she would always carry and would only add more heartache.

> Her bringing any action to expose her own father would only put her in a bad light in the eyes of the American public. I refuse to demand this of Peggy because I feel that it would only add torture to her confused state of mind. It's a pretty tragic mess, Your Honor, for a young girl to be entangled in. It is my contention Judge Scott, that these facts be presented to the court of the District Attorney by me and once these facts are presented, let the court deal with the parties involved, as it so deems.

I am at a loss to understand what is best in my procedure for the best interest of Peggy Ann's future Judge Scott, but having the utmost faith in your integrity as a man of justice I would follow any suggestion you may offer or see fit to make. Certainly, Judge Scott, there is cause for a suit for libel where this man is concerned, in the untold amount of damage that has been brought to her personal life and her career as well as definite criminal action to be filed.

Peggy Ann will be on the coast August 17 through the 30th and I am close by, having just arrived at the new Institution at Corona. Do you think that anything could be done in this interim? (This said business manager maintains his offices and operates in Beverly Hills.)

As Lincoln once said in other desperate circumstances, You are my last hope for a happy ending to my twenty-year-old daughter's future ... I pray with more intense fervor than ever before that you will be able to help me. For whatever advice that you see fit to give me, I shall be profoundly grateful.

Peggy and Richard had been visited only once by her father. Bill Garner stayed with them for one week, after which they put him on the train to Washington State "and that was that," Richard said. "Never saw him again."

Now Virginia was making a nervous wreck out of her daughter. She would call the Hayeses on the telephone, utterly drunk and making no sense. They felt a duty to her, wanting to be nice, and they had visited Virginia on occasion; but "she was a very difficult woman," said Richard. The fact that she refused to let go of the past and continually dwelled on wrongs she felt had been done to her made her a thorn in their sides.

"I still feel that Virginia had become a mental problem," wrote her mother, Mrs. Craig, to Bill Garner, "and I do think that she is trying very hard to make up for the mistakes that she made. I well understand Virginia's problems. I know what the drink does to some people and she was one who couldn't take it." Later, she made a request of Garner. "Is it true that you have sold the home? I am wondering if there is anything left. Virginia kept promising me that she would reimburse us and I kept sending her money all the time, the last amount that I sent her was $480.00 and then right after that she was picked up on that last offense and sentenced to that place. I gave better than three thousand dollars in the two years that Peggy was in New York. I do feel that I should be remembered with a little."

Probate Judge Condee had, indeed, approved the sale of Peggy's house for $30,000 to Mr. and Mrs. Albert G. Ruben. Of that amount, $8,500 went to pay off the mortgage.

The Hayes' formerly enchanted life was becoming troubled now. "We were too young," says Richard now in retrospect. They separated in April 1952.

Peggy was asked to appear on Kate Smith's show again. She obliged on April 22, acting in a dramatic sketch entitled "The Cure."

Virginia's check charges, for which she had been detained in the California Institution for Women, would be dismissed on October third of the next year.

CHAPTER 17

Nineteen fifty-three would be a very bad year for both Peggy and Virginia.

When Peggy turned twenty-one in February, she discovered that there was no money left in her trust fund. She was told that her mother had invested it, and the investments had gone bad. Many people blamed Virginia; Virginia blamed Bill Garner. He, after all, was the guardian of Peggy's property. Bill, however, might not have had any dishonorable intentions. Even Virginia later admitted that he had waived all fees due him as Peggy's guardian. He probably used the money in her trust to make the payments on her house as long as he could.

Yes, it was a bad year. Virginia's sister, Helen, committed suicide that year and, on October 13, Richard went to Juarez, Mexico, and obtained a divorce from Peggy. The grounds were incompatibility.

"I'm not the kind of a person who does not carry a grudge—I do," Richard said in a 2002 interview, "and I can't find anything in my soul at this stage of my life that I dislike [Peggy] for. We were just too young."

Her marriage over, Peggy was back on stage. Her new agent, Jerry Gershwin, also got her jobs in live television dramas. She soon appeared on the *Robert Montgomery Presents* episode called "Claire Ambler," as well as productions of *Studio One, Playhouse of Stars* and *Lux Video Theatre*. In 1952, she had returned to the New York City Center for a play entitled *First Lady*. When that had completed its run, she and her pal Roddy McDowall toured with *The Youngest*. For a week in February 1953, Peggy reprised her role in *The Pick-Up Girl* at the Empress Playhouse in St. Louis. The following week, her friend Margaret O'Brien would appear there in *Peg O' My Heart*. It was a small world.

During the summer, Peggy appeared at the Saratoga Spa Summer Theatre in the play *The Moon is Blue*. While in the area, she was interviewed by Martha Brooks of radio station WGY in Schenectady.

The press seemed eager to bring Peggy's love life back to the forefront, and, indeed, she was telling them that what she wanted most was marriage and a houseful of children.

The September thirteenth issue of *Inside TV* presented a photo of Peggy Ann with fellow former child star Jackie Cooper at the Stork Club. Rumors were flying about these two, and the October issue of *TV Show* featured a two-page photo spread of their weekend at the Catskills. Was there really a romance brewing between them? What a great story that would make— two former child stars fall in love! Maybe they would have a storybook wedding and beget little child stars of their own. The press wanted to believe that this was a serious relationship. Whether it was or not is uncertain. Even though Peggy and Jackie were seen together often and also appeared in a play in San Francisco together, there was nary a word written about her in Cooper's future autobiography entitled *Please Don't Shoot My Dog*.

Pictured with fellow former-child-star Jackie Cooper at the Stork Club. Rumors were flying about these two.

Marriage over, Peggy's dating again. Seen here with Eddie Fisher.

From the time she was fifteen, reporters had been linking Peggy with one eligible bachelor after another, from Lon McCallister to Tab Hunter. She was friendly to all but it seems that the right man just hadn't come along yet.

One thing that might be noticed in photos that were taken of Peggy at this stage of her life is that she no longer had the cute upturned nose that she had had as a child. It was now straighter, so cosmetic surgery had obviously occurred at some point prior to this. Says researcher-writer Laura Wagner, "I don't think she was happy with her face." Nevertheless, photographers thought she looked fine and she had always been asked to appear in magazine advertisements, the latest of which was for Sacony.

Having such a busy work and social life, it is no wonder that Peggy was stopped more than once for speeding. In 1953, she was given a ticket for speeding on the Henry Hudson Parkway. Three months later, she was again stopped by the police, this time for speeding in a restricted area and double-parking. Peggy had been out of town when it was time to respond to the summons, so nothing was done about them. Consequently, the magistrate signed a warrant for her arrest on sight. This resulted in her being taken to court and fined fifty-five dollars. The solemnity of the experience had a jarring effect on her. "I have never been so scared in my

The camera caught a tired Peggy after a long day.

life," she said as she left the courthouse in March 1954.

Even though Peggy wasn't able to see B, her childhood stand-in, much anymore, she kept in touch enough to know when B had married and started a family. When B's baby was born, her old buddy "Pan" sent a very nice baby gift and signed the card with her nickname.

B looks back sadly at Peggy's career since *A Tree Grows in Brooklyn*. "I thought that they weren't utilitizing Peggy's talent at all because I do know she was a talented person," she says. "She had such depth and she was such a smart person. She had the capacity to really understand a role and she was very serious about it."

Later that year, producers were casting the play *Bus Stop*. This was a play that would be tested in Philadelphia before hitting Broadway. How Peggy yearned for the leading role of Cherie! For a while, it seemed that the part was hers. Playwright William Inge told her she was his first choice. When the final decision was announced, however, it was Kim Stanley who got the role. Peggy was heartbroken. Not one to wallow in self-pity, however, she returned to Broadway in *Home is the Hero* at the Booth Theatre.

Home is the Hero's author, Walter Macken, played the lead, and costarring with them were Glenda Farrell, J. Pat O'Malley, Art Smith, Frances Fuller, Ann Thomas, Donald Harron, Loretta Leversee, and Christopher Plummer. In this story, Mr. Macken's character, Paddo O'Reilly, returns home after serving five years in jail for murdering his best friend in a drunken brawl. Once home, he discovers that his wife has started drinking and taking in boarders, his daughter (Peggy) is dating a rakish gambler, and his son has proposed to the daughter of the man O'Reilly had murdered. The man attempts to bully his family into submission, reopens old wounds when he tries to apologize to his victim's widow, then, when he almost kills again, leaves the family, to the relief of all.

The production received nice advance publicity, but failed to live up to expectations. Reviews were unanimously negative. Brooks Atkinson, in the September 24, 1955 *New York Times*, wrote "With one or two exceptions the characters are uninteresting. The writing is pedestrian. There is no vitality under the surface bickering of the story. In comparison with the turbulent quarrels in the O'Casey plays, the tone of *Home is the Hero* is pedantic. Mr. Macken goes through the familiar motions, but the fire is not there." Of Peggy, he said "Peggy Ann Garner gives an uncommonly skillful characterization of a confused and unhappy girl." Even though the play left much to be desired, Peggy's talent was still as good as ever and much appreciated. *Home is the Hero* lasted for less than a month, closing on October sixteenth. *Variety* reported that, after a 29-performance subscription run, it closed to a loss of about $30,000.

During this time, Peggy was living in an apartment at 47 East 61st Street in New York City, but she would soon be going west again. Nunnally Johnson, the *Pied Piper* screenwriter, had expanded the scope of his career. He was now to produce and direct a Twentieth Century-Fox film called *Black Widow*, and he asked Peggy to take a color test for an important role in it. Scheduling such a test was not easy. Peggy was in rehearsal for a television show until 5:00, so Johnson had a hairdresser meet her at her apartment at 5:30 and they did the test early the next morning. A day later, he offered her the part. Peggy was measured for her wardrobe on Sunday, spent Monday at the television studio, the hairdresser came over to her apartment that night, and early Tuesday they shot Peggy's two New York scenes. The rest would have to be done in Hollywood—but not yet. Peggy had to fly to Brazil first for a previously-scheduled personal appearance commitment. A week later, she was able to fly to Hollywood to finish working on the movie.

This role was different from her earlier ones. No longer was Peggy the cherubic child moviegoers remembered from earlier Twentieth Century-Fox movies. In this film, she was a young lady. Not a kind, gentle young lady, but a schemer. What a wonderful opportunity to show her versatility!

When Peggy and the picture's star George Raft were interviewed, he recalled their earlier project. "In 1943, we were in *Nob Hill* together. I used to help her with her school lessons between takes."

"But I passed anyway," Peggy quipped with a grin.

It was nice to be back in California again and to see many of her old friends. How she loved that place!

Peggy appeared twice in a single issue of *Photoplay*. Both spots plugged her new movie. On page 11 was a photo from a scene she and Ginger Rogers did together, with a description of the film. Then on page 57, Peggy is shown modeling a low-waisted coat dress as she admires a fringe-topped Hillmann Minx convertible. Only a very slim lady would look attractive in this dress, so Peggy was the perfect choice. This spot, too, mentioned *Black Widow*. This would run in the January 1955 issue to coincide with the release of *Black Widow*.

Once the work and promos for this film were done and Peggy was back in New York, she bumped into Jackie Cooper and his new wife, Barbara, who were there on vacation. Peggy and Jackie were again photographed together as he took center stage, playing the drums at Lil Brown's Hotel in Loch Sheldrake as Peggy looked on in support, smiling broadly. They would also be seen and photographed as Jackie took Peggy for a spin in a convertible.

Virginia was paroled on October 27, 1954. She didn't stay in California long, though. Her daughter was in New York, and that's where she wanted to be, too; so off to New York she went.

Reporter Doug McClelland interviewed Peggy for the *Newark Sun-*

With Ginger Rogers in *Black Widow*.

Taking a spin with Jackie.

day News. It had been in Newark that she lived for a while as a small child, so the newspaper had a special interest in this young lady. The result was a nice two-page article about her in their November 21 issue. There were four photos of Peggy in various stages of her life, the largest of which was a recent one of her in an evening gown and looking absolutely gorgeous. The title, "A Child Star Grows Up," concurred with what that photo already told us. This interview had taken place at her Manhattan apartment. Reporter McClelland noted that Peggy now had brown eyes and pale blonde hair. They talked about Peggy's apartment. She had painted it herself, she said, and was planning on buying some antiques for it. She pointed out to Doug the gold statuette on the mantel over her fireplace and said proudly, "I got Oscar, my favorite boyfriend, for *A Tree*." When asked of her hopes for the future, Peggy said that she would really enjoy doing a musical comedy someday, but her most cherished dream was for a happy marriage that produces lots of children.

Virginia was in trouble again. In December, she was arrested under the name of Louise Hallie in New York for another worthless $300 check. She was sent to the Rockland State [Mental] Hospital in Orangeburg, New York, registered under the same fictitious name. She had been grieving the separation from Peggy that the industry had forced upon her, they were told, and the hospital was to treat what was thought to have been a nervous breakdown. This was apparently not the case, though, and they kept wondering "Why are you here? Who sent you?" Feeling that she was perfectly rational, they soon released her. The following January, the check charge was dismissed. Later that same month, Virginia was arrested again while in New York. She was held without bail on a fugitive charge related to her 1952 sentence, from which she had been on parole. She liked being in jail, she told reporters, because she was treated better there than in the outside world. Of course, she was quick to let her fellow inmates know who her famous daughter was, and that gave her the respect she craved.

To quote *With the Dream Came a Curse*, written by Virginia's nephew, Vince DeVito, Jr.:

> On several occasions, Virginia contributed to making matters worse by using unbalanced methods in a frustrated state of mind while under great stress when she purposely violated the law as a means to divulge her story in court. But what remains without a doubt is this woman's sanity. In fact, the question that arises is how she maintained her sanity throughout her entire life in the face of such adversity.

As always, Virginia's parents went to bat for her. They wrote a letter to Judge Scott on April 5, 1955, in which they pleaded with him to help straighten out all the wrongs that had been done to their daughter throughout the years, to help make things right again. The Craigs had spent all their savings to help her and they felt she was still being treated unfairly, having been committed to Bellevue Hospital and jailed at Corona. Neither they nor Virginia blamed Peggy for any of Virginia's misfortunes. Rather, they thought it was the entertainment industry's moguls and Peggy's managers who were at fault. They felt that Peggy was just as much a victim as Virginia was. What hurt so much was that those people had led Peggy to believe that Virginia had squandered all her money. The Craigs felt sure that it was Bill Garner who did that, not Virginia. But Peggy was now alienated enough from Virginia that she wouldn't cooperate in bringing justice to the guilty parties. Because Peggy was an adult now, it was necessary to get her cooperation if anything was to be done.

In the meantime, Peggy played the female lead opposite Jackie Cooper for six weeks in a play entitled *John Loves Mary*. This show was mounted at the United Nations Theatre (formerly the Alcazar Theater) in San Francisco. Also in the cast were Lee Patrick, Harry Carey, Jr, Tom Powers, and San Francisco bandleader, Del Courtney.

"I played the part of a Red Cross worker who came over from London to the United States and became very involved with the American Red Cross, so I had a lot of lines with both Jackie Cooper and Peggy Ann

JACKIE COOPER and PEGGY ANN GARNER in "JOHN LOVES MARY"

UNITED NATIONS THEATRE
Formerly

Alcazar

THE PLAYGOER

Co-starring with Jackie in *John Loves Mary*.

Garner," says Courtney. "Some people said there was some kind of a romance going on between Peggy Ann and Jackie Cooper, but there wasn't really."

From an early age, Peggy had always seemed to charm her co-stars. She never lost that ability. "Peggy Ann Garner was a delight to work with and very pleasant," Del says. "She was always very friendly and very sociable. She was always up." He said that offstage, Jackie was the center of attention while Peggy took a subordinate role. It was Jackie who was considered the star. "And he deserves it. He's a very talented guy and a good actor, a good performer."

Once the play closed, Peggy's next project was an April 7, 1955 *Best of Broadway* telecast on CBS. This show included the TV adaptation of the play *Stage Door*, in which Peggy gave a marvelous performance. She also made appearances on *Climax, Studio One,* and *Stage 7* in rapid succession.

On August 17, Virginia filed a criminal complaint in San Mateo County Superior Court against Donald Hellbush for fraud, perjury and obstruction of Virginia's constitutional rights. Shortly after, she requested a writ of habeas corpus because she had been in custody at the California Institute for Women for more than two years. She claimed this incarceration was illegal, unlawful and felonious, based on fraud and grand theft of legal documents seized illegally without a search warrant.

Judge Scott was unimpressed. He denied the writ on September 20 because she had pled guilty by reason of insanity. Once she was found by two doctors to be sane, that automatically changed the plea to guilty. Good try, but no cigar.

Upon hearing Judge Scott's verdict, Virginia enlisted the help of her friend Marion Terry, asking her to request, as President of the Parents of Motion Picture Children, a complete investigation of this case. Mrs. Terry complied.

In the meantime, Peggy was finally able to try again for *Bus Stop*. Playwright Inge had invited her to read for it again now that a national tour was being planned. This time the competition wasn't as stiff, and she was finally awarded the coveted part of Cherie. "Usually, I'm a terrible reader," Peggy told Margaret Harford of the *Mirror-News*. "I think most actors are. But Mr. Inge put me at ease so quickly I think I could have won the part reading the Gettysburg Address." Peggy couldn't suppress her excitement. Not only would she be doing the role for which she'd yearned for a year,

She's just plain beautiful.

but her salary would give her enough money to finish paying off her mother's debts that had been incurred as Peggy was growing up.

Her leading man, she was told, would be Albert Salmi. That just couldn't be, she thought. Brooklyn-born Salmi was the man who was winning rave notices and awards for his work in this very same role on Broadway. A conscientious member of the Actor's Studio, he had been proclaimed the Toast of Broadway because of his stunning performance in *Bus Stop*, and the Broadway play was still running. Why on earth would he want to leave that to go on tour? The prospect of working with such an accomplished actor was frightening to her.

Salmi loved New York, but had grown restless and wanted to take this topnotch tour of the country. Once he and Peggy met and began

PEGGY ANN GARNER and ALBERT SALMI in "BUS STOP"

STAGEBILL

For the SELWYN THEATRE

Her *Bus Stop* leading man on this tour was Broadway's Albert Salmi.

working together, her fears dissipated. He was a giant of a man, tall and brawny, but he was also a kind, gentle man who treated her with respect. The biggest surprise was that this big Broadway star was so quiet and reserved. Albert Salmi seemed too good to be true—so real, so unpretentious. What an oddity he was!

The tour began in Central City, Colorado, and it was there that Peggy and Albert first became intimate. Behind closed doors, their romance blossomed.

On stage, too, her life was going well. The Central City audiences loved Peggy. The tour would be going to Los Angeles soon, and an *L. A. Times* reporter interviewed Peggy over the telephone. "What a wonderful experience we've had here in Central City!" Peggy said enthusiastically. "It's so historic. There are people here of the fifth generation. Whenever we have time off, we go up into the real Rockies for fishing, hiking and horseback riding. I guess I'll get used to the altitude, but I'm slow about it. Sometimes I turn up breathless on the stage and not from stage fright either."

Their next stop was Los Angeles, but this audience gave her a cooler reception. "When the curtain fell on opening night," Peggy told the *Mirror-News*, "I turned to the others on stage and said, 'Where's the gun?' I guess we're spoiled. At the Central City Festival in Colorado, all you had to do was say 'hello' and the audience got hysterical." The resulting write-up in the magazine *Plays and Players* was kind only to Albert. It said that Peggy's acting was amateurish. How hurtful that was!

From Los Angeles, the troupe went to San Francisco, then Chicago for an indefinite run. Next came Kansas City, St. Louis, and various cities in Ohio.

Except for a brief time at their Chicago engagement, in which his former girlfriend showed up and spent quite a bit of time with him, Peggy and Albert were considered by their fellow thespians to be a couple. During the eleven months that they toured together, Peggy fell in love with Albert. To be married to a man like him would bring normality into her life. She couldn't remember ever having that.

Christmas Day was spent on a train, but Peggy didn't care. She was in love. And being in love made her happier about everything. She soon wrote a letter to her mother from the Netherland Plaza Hotel in Cincinnati:

Dearest Mother:

I hope with all my heart you find it in <u>your</u> heart to forgive a most errant daughter for not writing. Excuses I cannot give for full pardon—but really, the past 6 months I've been all over the country, working harder than ever before—and getting all my bills paid, and beginning to feel a bit secure for the first time in a while.

This letter cannot possibly cover the past 6 months, but it does bring a promise of letters (often) to come in the future.

We're here for a week, Mumps, then (here is the schedule) Jan. 16-17-18 Dayton—at the Victory Theatre, Jan. 19-20-21 Columbus (Hartman Theatre), Jan. 23-28 Cleveland (Hanna Theatre), Jan. 30—Feb. 11 Detroit (Shubert Theatre), then Baltimore, Washington, Boston, etc. I'll send the exact dates when I have them.

I hope you got my Xmas packages. Daddy said you sent me a package, which hasn't caught up with me yet. I saw him for a couple of days in Chicago. We left there Xmas day, and spent it on a train. Next year, Mother, we *will* be together, I hope and pray.

If any of your things don't fit, send them to Bonwits in Chicago, and they'll exchange them.

That's all for now, Mother, as I must go to the theatre. I'll see all the folks in Cleveland.

Write soon—to one of our theatres. I don't know the hotels, so it's safest to write at the theatre. If it misses me, it will always be forwarded.

I know it seems difficult at times to believe, Mother (but I don't mean to make it that way), but you are always in my heart and thoughts.

All my love,
Peggy

Peggy was hoping this play would be a turning point that would enable her to return for good to Hollywood.

H. G. Robinson, Deputy Director of the Office of the Attorney General in San Francisco, sent a letter to Marion Terry. He reported that they reviewed Virginia's criminal complaint against Donald Hellbush and Judge Scott's denial of her request for a writ of habeas corpus. Dated January 25, 1956, this letter said, in part:

> Under the provisions of Penal Code Section 1192 the court, in determining the degree of the offense, stated that Mrs. Garner came into San Mateo county and within a few days began writing fictitious checks all signed by fictitious names as she had no account in any bank. Her method was to go to a store and buy women's merchandise and then have someone else return it for a refund but some of the merchandise she obtained was never recovered. She has had divorce problems with her husband and problems concerning the business affairs of her daughter in the movies. She explains her predicament by saying she thought if she willfully wrote these checks and was arrested it would bring the unjust treatment she had received before the court. She was examined by two alienists hired by the State and by two hired by herself, who stated that while she was not insane, she was badly in need of psychopathic help.
>
> With respect to her violation of the terms of her parole, it appears that she failed to keep her parole officer informed of her whereabouts at all times. She left the State of California without permission and her whereabouts was unknown until information was received from the New York Police Department on January 13, 1955, advising that she had been placed in the Rockland State Hospital. She apparently came to the attention of the New York authorities as a result of her arrest on December 3, 1954, on suspicion of forgery.
>
> Investigation was also conducted by this office at the California Institution for Women, where the subject is regarded as a model inmate. Mrs. Garner was also interviewed by agents of this office in an attempt to find some avenue through which this office could be of assistance to her, in accordance with your request.
>
> After a full review of the matter it appears that Mrs. Garner acknowledges the violations of which she stands convicted and also acknowledges the violation of the terms of her parole. Under the circumstances this office must accept the findings of the

court and the parole authorities. This is indeed an unfortunate case but it is believed that the most objective program can be found in the comments by Dr. James E. McGinnis, consulting psychiatrist, who examined Mrs. Garner on September 24, 1955. He stated:

> "She appears capable of achieving success on her own in the field of her choice if she could utilize her energies entirely in this direction, and if she were able to relinquish her past entanglement with the affairs of her daughter. Perhaps she eventually may do this."

It is further noted that the Board of Trustees of the Corona Institution will undoubtedly grant Mrs. Garner another parole at their next meeting with the stipulation that she does not leave the State of California. If such eventuality comes to pass, may we earnestly suggest that you prevail upon Mrs. Garner, as a friend, to comply with the terms of such parole.

It was right before the troupe's Boston stop that Albert's contract expired and he did not opt to renew it. Instead, he returned to his beloved New York; Dick York took over his role on the road. Dick was a fine actor, but it just wasn't the same to Peggy without Albert.

While the play was being presented in Boston, she developed symptoms that led her to believe that she was pregnant. Peggy knew Albert was the only one who could be the baby's father. She telephoned him in New York and gave him the news.

Albert was not pleased with this turn of events, but did what he felt was right—he agreed to marry Peggy.

As their wedding was being planned, Salmi brought a couple of his actor friends, R. G. Armstrong and Pat Hingle, over to enjoy Peggy's cooking. It's true that he was basically a very sweet, caring man, but Albert had been raised in the Finnish tradition. Both of his parents had been natives of Finland, and his father had ruled their home with an iron hand. Albert now adopted his father's ways, treating Peggy as if she were a servant. From the time he came in with Armstrong and Hingle, it was "get me this" and "get me that."

For much of Peggy's life, she had been manipulated by people, but she had no intention of allowing that to happen now. After good-naturedly playing along with Albert for a while, she then put her foot down. "Get you! Get it yourself!" she said. No longer would she be subservient to him. This marriage would be a fifty-fifty proposition.

At first, Albert didn't know what to make of it. After a while, however, he adjusted and things became smoother. In the meantime, his two friends felt reassured that this would indeed be a good marriage. Peggy could handle Albert just fine.

Wanting to get started on the right foot, Peggy gave her future mother-in-law, Ida Salmi, a lovely gift of Evening in Paris perfume. Ida had been widowed eleven years earlier and had lived a life very similar to that of Peggy's screen mother in *A Tree Grows in Brooklyn*—she lived in a Brooklyn apartment house and, as Albert was growing up, she had cleaned houses for a living. Peggy wanted hard-working Ida to have a little luxury in her life.

Barbara Whiting recalls making a trip during this time with Albert, Peggy, and an agent-friend to Tijuana, Mexico, to see a bullfight. Before they left home, Barbara's mother had firmly instructed, "Don't eat any greens! Stay away from all that stuff." Perhaps there was still a bit of the rebel in the girls, however, for they did indeed enjoy salads while there. The result, Barbara says, was that her doctor "got a great deal of business after we got home. I got sick. Peggy got sick."

They recovered in plenty of time for the wedding, though.

Being married in a church was important to Peggy so, even though neither of them was a member of the First Presbyterian Church in Manhattan, they had their wedding in its main sanctuary on May 18, 1956. This was twenty-eight-year-old Albert's first marriage and twenty-four-year-old Peggy's second. Her maid of honor was agent Ina Bernstein. To Ina, Peggy gave a beautiful 14-carat gold calendar charm with an amethyst marking the big day and "Albert and Peggy" engraved on the back. About forty guests were there to help them celebrate on that very special Friday.

After honeymooning in Jamaica, the couple returned home to New York. Now maybe her dreams would come true. Being a good wife and mother was more important to her than all the acting jobs in the world.

Albert was quite thrifty, which is said to be another characteristic common to the Finnish culture. Peggy was usually a conservative spender as well. As a result, when Peggy's Aunt Jeanne and Uncle Vince DeVito visited their apartment, they found it to be quite a simple place. It consisted of just a large open room for living and sleeping, and an enclosed alcove for the kitchen. "These are Broadway stars," Vince thought to himself. "Surely they could afford better." He and Albert were silent, however, while Peggy Ann and her Aunt Jeanne carried on a lively conversation.

The newlyweds shared a love of acting, and they were both exceptionally good at it. Peggy turned down jobs that would keep her away from her husband, opting for live TV dramas like *Show of the Month* and *Kraft Theatre* instead, but Albert was accepting work regardless of location. One live television drama he did with Paul Newman that year would become a classic—*The U.S. Steel Hour's* presentation of "Bang the Drum Slowly." At this stage of his life, Albert was receiving award after award for his work.

Peggy's stage work was now receiving special recognition as well. That same year, she was presented with the Hasty Pudding's theatrical award as their "Woman of the Year." According to the Hasty Pudding's website, this award was created "to honor artists who have made 'a lasting and impressive contribution to the world of entertainment.'" This was only the sixth year of its existence, and Peggy could now take her place with Gertrude Lawrence, Barbara Bel Geddes, Mamie Eisenhower, Shirley Booth and Debbie Reynolds, who had won this honor in previous years.

The traditional schedule for the Hasty Pudding presentations begins with a parade down the streets of Harvard Square, in which the honored woman rides at the head. Once they reach 12 Holyoke Street, where the Hasty Pudding Theatricals are held, they gather in the auditorium. The woman's glorious achievements are spotlighted, then she is called up to the stage for a roast, in which her not-so-glorious achievements are brought to the attention of all. She is presented with her award and shown a preview of the show to come. Later, cocktails are served, followed by dinner in her honor and a party.

A very sympathetic article ran in the December 4, 1956 *Herald Express* about Virginia. Reporter Dick Walton states that Virginia was released from Corona women's prison earlier in the year and was now full of remorse. "This will be the seventh straight Christmas without Peggy," she told him. "More than anything else for Christmas, I want to be reconciled or reunited with my daughter." Living now in a cheap Hollywood apartment on N. Vine Street, Virginia continued with dramatic flair, "Accuse me of the things of which I'm guilty, but don't crucify me for things I didn't do. I want Peg to realize her mother isn't a complete no-good." Virginia swore that she didn't drink anymore and was rehabilitated. "Nobody can ever say I was anything but a good mother to her."

The next year Peggy received the answer to her prayers. Following a mere four-hour labor, Peggy and Albert's baby daughter was born on March 30, 1957—ten months after her parents' wedding. They named her Catherine Ann Salmi. Her initials soon became her nickname, and they called her "Cas." This had been a precarious pregnancy, and Cas was born three weeks early. She was a small baby, weighing in at five pounds fifteen ounces, but her health appeared to be good.

To commemorate the blessed event, Peggy's friend B sent her a gold medal with "To PAN'S CAS" engraved on the reverse side.

Peggy and Albert had each been an only child, so neither knew any-

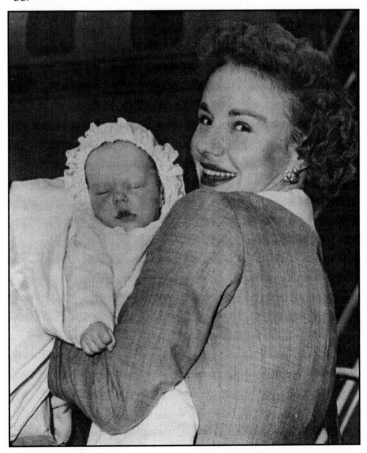

The fulfillment of Peggy's fondest dream—a baby of her own. She was named after Peggy's Aunt Catherine. [Photofest]

thing about caring for babies. Because of Cas' tiny size, Peggy was afraid to bathe her at first, so Albert did it. It was his Actor's Studio friend Pat Hingle who taught him how to care for a baby, and Albert then took an active part in fatherhood.

This little child seemed to be exactly what Peggy needed. The couple didn't know Virginia's whereabouts when the blessed event occurred, but three weeks later, they did. Peggy then wrote to her mother, excitedly relaying the news of Cas' birth. She and Albert were taking shifts, she said, one sleeping while the other cared for little Cas.

The golden-haired, blue-eyed child grew to look more and more like her daddy every day. Peggy affectionately called her "Kitten" and wrote to her mother what a good baby she was, though "full of the devil." Peggy was a devoted mother, not wanting to interrupt little Cas' sleeping and feeding schedule, even when they went on vacation.

Now that Albert had wowed Broadway and received such acclaim for his live-television work, his next step seemed to be movies. Many were offered to him, but he turned them down. Film, he felt, was inferior to the live stage. As he would sometimes quote Lee Strasberg, "Movies are not art." Albert's heart was forever on the New York stage.

Then a movie role was offered that he simply could not pass up—that of Smerdjakov in the classic *The Brothers Karamazov*. He had been flying out to California now and then to do television jobs, but he would be staying there for a few months this time, so MGM put him up in a studio apartment in Los Angeles. He enjoyed the work, but was glad when it was over so he could go back home to New York and his little family. California just wasn't his cup of tea.

Such an exceptional job did Albert do in that film that MGM wanted to nominate him for an Oscar in the supporting-actor category. Director Richard Brooks advised him to decline the nomination. Winning it would be the "kiss of death" for his career, he said. Albert took that advice and turned it down. Later, he would regret it.

Peggy and Albert's social life was quite busy these days as their friends would drop by frequently. One couple they both enjoyed was Mark and Helen Richman. "They would come to our place for dinner," says Mark. "We had an apartment in New York on West 20th Street." After having worked together in *End As a Man*, the men saw each other often at the Actor's Studio and elsewhere. He recalls that Albert was "a good-natured, warm, open fellow." Then he added, "We all adored Albert. He was like a big teddybear." Of Peggy, he says, "I loved Peggy. Peggy was a wonderful actress and a terrific gal, and I remember her terrific laugh and smile." Peggy was proud of their daughter and enjoyed showing her to their friends. "She was a lovely little girl," says Mark. "She was a pale little blonde, lovely girl, very well-dressed out."

The friendship that had developed between Peggy and Barbara Whiting when they were children working in films together had endured through the years. They were still keeping in touch with each other. "Barbara Whiting is in Europe with the U.S.O. and having a wonderful look at the world," Peggy wrote to her mother. "Before this, she went to Alaska and the islands, gained 8 pounds, and looks better than she has in years."

Albert's career was now going extremely well. Film and television offers were plentiful. Peggy, on the other hand, was in less demand by the film industry. She was cast in quite a few television shows, which helped out with the family expenses, but the quality of roles in films that she had had as a child was never to be hers again.

It seemed that Albert was always away. His acting jobs were so often at locations away from their home city. When Peggy wasn't able to go with him, they would write each other loving letters, but she missed him. Peggy knew she shouldn't complain, however, because she understood that it wasn't his idea to travel—it's just a necessary part of his work. He wanted to be a good provider for his family and he truly loved his work.

Peggy was becoming homesick for California and wanted to move back there. Albert, however, loved New York and wanted to stay where they were. That was his home and where his widowed mother lived. Peggy reasoned that their job opportunities would be better in California, and maybe he would be away from home less if they lived there. Salaries were much higher in the west, too, and live television on the east coast was on its way out. He relented, and they moved to Los Angeles.

They rented houses in the Brentwood section for a while. Peggy wrote about it to her mother, who was now living in San Francisco: "We have a lovely house, with a wonderful backyard, which will be great for the baby in the summertime. If summer ever comes! I'm beginning to wonder, with all of this rain. We're on the corner of San Vicente and Burlingame in Brentwood, and we have flowers and a few fruit trees, which Albert loves. I looked at about 30 houses before finding this one, but it was worth waiting for."

The Salmis rented a beautiful home on Burlingame in Los Angeles.

Peggy was back home in California now, but one important part of it was gone: Barbara had married and moved to Michigan. Many of her other friends were still here, though, and it was nice to have Albert at home in the evenings.

She was soon visited by a dear friend—B. How great it was to see her again! "She had a lovely home," says B. "My aunt and uncle lived in Hollywood at the time, so could babysit with my kids. Peggy really got upset at my not bringing them with me." Regarding Albert, she says, "I was surprised at Peggy being married to such a BIG guy. She seemed so in love and I was so very happy for her." (By now, Albert knew better than to tell Peggy to fetch things for him.)

Because he had spent most of his life in New York, where public transportation was abundant, Albert did not have a driver's license. Consequently, Peggy arose at six o'clock each morning to take him to work, then would pick him up at the end of the day. It was at the end of the last day of filming his second picture, *The Bravados*, that Albert was running to the car, tripped and fell, breaking his dominant left arm in two places. After putting it into a cast, the doctor gave him pills for the pain, but they did little good. "I feel so badly," Peggy wrote her mother, "as there is nothing I can do for him."

While the passage of time helped him feel better, no doubt, an award did, too. It was presented to him by The National Board of Review for his work in *The Brothers Karamazov* and *The Bravados*.

Peggy was delighted when, in July of 1958, Albert's arm was healed and they were both cast in a *Westinghouse Studio One* production called "Man Under Glass." It was nice to be working with her husband again, doing what they both did so well. When they were together, life was so much better.

In September, Albert was off again to begin rehearsals for the title role in the Broadway play *Howie*. Peggy and little Cas went with him. He was so happy to be back on the Broadway stage. Being in New York again made him realize how much he loved this place. How he yearned to move back! This, to him, was home.

One evening, Albert learned that someone very special was in the audience. It was Irja Helen Sandstrom's teenager daughter, Nancy. The Sandstroms had taken care of him when he was only four, while his mother worked during the summer, and he now welcomed Nancy backstage. She found him "humble and sincere, which I attribute to the nature of a Finn, the characteristic that struck me on my trips to Finland as well as with my associations with Finns in this country. I remember, too, when I complimented him on his acting talents that he commented that Peggy was the real talent, having been in the business much longer than he." Nancy was quite impressed with this man, who seemed so far removed emotionally from Hollywood. "He felt that a marriage relationship was so important, and he was so hopeful that this marriage would be lifelong," she says. Nancy would remember that visit fondly for a very long time.

Once the play was over and they returned to California, Albert renewed his efforts to talk Peggy into a move back east. It just wouldn't be practical, she felt. Their careers are here in California.

Some of Albert's friends were starting to move west, too. Paul Newman and his wife, Joanne Woodward, were now living there, and they invited the Salmis to dinner at their rented home. Peggy's buddy Barbara and their mutual agent-friend were invited with them, and they had a marvelous time. The salad that Paul had made for them was elegant in its simplicity and made extra-special by its dressing, which he had also made. "We have remembered that all our lives," Barbara says. No one there knew that this was a preview of things to come—the very popular salad dressings that would be marketed decades later under the Newman's Own label, with profits given to charity.

By October, Virginia was not having nearly as much fun as her daughter was. She was again in jail, this time in Franklin County. She tried to arrange to have representatives of the media come so she could reveal all

The best portraits of Peggy were taken by Roddy McDowall.

to them, but they did not show up. She assumed that meant the guards would not let them in.

Once she was out on parole, Virginia immediately got in trouble. On November 7, she was charged with leaving her residence without the knowledge and consent of her parole agent, suspicion of forgery, and, with her whereabouts unknown, failure to comply with parole rules. By January 30, 1959, she had been located and brought before the Board of Trustees. The actions they took were written up as "Denied charges; revoked; term redetermined and fixed at 9 years on each of 5 Cts. CC; parole consideration postponed indefinitely."

Albert was cast in the MGM film *The Unforgiven* as the beau of young Audrey Hepburn's character. This picture would be filmed in Mexico during the spring of 1959. Even though Peggy was pregnant again, she went with him. Her husband was fond of children and she knew that a second child would make him happy. While in Mexico, however, she developed a severe case of dysentery and lost the baby. The couple was heartbroken.

Once filming was over, it was back to New York, where Albert was cast in the play *The Failures*. He brought his little family along.

"It is extremely hot in NY now," wrote Peggy to her mother in June. "Summer is really here, with the high humidity. Albert is fine, and the baby grows lovelier and dearer every day. We have no new pictures of her, but Albert has promised to take some soon."

Peggy's acting was put on the back burner for a while so she could spend most of her time with her husband and caring for little Cas. She did work occasionally, however. Her letter to Virginia continues, "I'm doing a *U.S. Steel Show* on the 29th of July, so watch, if you can." [This was the episode entitled "We Wish on the Moon."] Motherhood was wonderful, but Peggy still enjoyed acting jobs when they didn't take her away from her little family for too long.

With this letter, she enclosed some head-and-shoulder portraits of herself wearing a lacy, off-the-shoulder dress. "These pictures were taken last week by Roddy [McDowall] and I'm very pleased at the way they turned out," she wrote. "Please let me know if you like them." They were, indeed, beautiful. McDowall was not only a gifted actor, but also a fabulous photographer. Of all the portraits taken of Peggy throughout her life, his were the best. They were obviously taken with love.

Early in December, Peggy received a twenty-eight-page handwritten letter from her mother. Virginia was pouring out her heart to her daughter. Ever since that confrontation with Ed Sullivan ten years earlier, Peggy had behaved coolly toward Virginia when they were together. Her letters to Virginia these days were superficially cheerful, but they were few and far between. There was a chasm now between mother and daughter that not even time had been able to mend. Peggy had never brought her toddler-daughter to see Virginia; it was only when Virginia took the initiative, that she was able to see little Cas. Twice, she had come to visit the Salmis. When she did, Peggy greeted her with very little warmth; it was Albert who would offer Virginia coffee and try to make her feel welcome.

Virginia now wanted to get everything out into the open. She wanted answers. She wanted them to reach a level of understanding so she could have peace of mind and they could enjoy a close relationship once again.

Her health depended on it, she said. "I have many times since wished we had never seen Hollywood and stayed in Canton, Ohio. All this grief may have been avoided," she wrote.

Fortunately, however, the bad feelings that had previously existed between Virginia and Bill Garner had been smoothed over. He was now a tremendous help to his ex-wife, dealing with the parole board for her and paying her medical bills.

At this point, though, Peggy had enough problems of her own without having to worry about her mother's too. Ever since they had returned home after doing *Howie*, Albert had been campaigning to move back to New York. Peggy resisted. While she was telling reporters that she believed the husband should be the undisputed head of the household, her wants and needs carried just as much weight as Albert's. She wanted to stay in California. Heated arguments ensued, which would upset Peggy so much that her neck muscles would become very tense and sore.

If one is renting a house in California, he can easily pick up and go back to New York. There's no major commitment, no setting down of roots. Nevertheless, Peggy prevailed and the couple now bought a house on Bundy Drive—in California.

Peggy especially liked this portrait, which was also taken by Roddie McDowall. (From the collection of the DeVito family)

The frustrations and resentments continued.

Late in 1960, Albert, Peggy, and Cas were mentioned in a book entitled *Siirtokansan Kalenteri*, which was newly-published in Finland. The title meant "Immigrants' Calendar" and it contained interviews of people who had migrated from Finland to other countries, then achieved success. While the true immigrants in Albert's family had been his parents, he was the one spotlighted in the book. After talking with Albert about his work and family, interviewer Lahja Maria Koskinen then contacted his mother Ida, who said (in Finnish), "Although my daughter-in-law is a

In 1960, Peggy was given a star on the Hollywood Walk of Fame. (From the collection of Jeff Howard)

noted child star and movie star, she is a modest and sweet girl, and I am a fortunate and satisfied mother, because I have good children who look after my best interests and, in addition, little Catherine Ann. They all love me." Indeed, Peggy and Albert both had an abundance of love for his mother.

Peggy's mother wasn't feeling nearly as loved as Albert's was. Marion Terry had been Virginia's strong ally throughout her trials and tribulations. It was to Marion Virginia wrote in March that she was on the verge of committing suicide. Marion, of course, hastened to write back, encouraging her to keep fighting and not to give up.

Virginia would soon find someone else to love her.

CHAPTER 18

Nineteen Sixty-one was a year of change for both Peggy and her mother.

Virginia had come out of her despair and remarried early this year. Her new husband, Clarence Swainston, was the owner of Big Bear Lumber Company in San Mateo County, California, and the father of two grown children. Clarence soon lost his business, however, and there was a lawsuit involved that caused the Swainston couple much grief. Virginia blamed Ray Moulin, Clarence's children, and State officials, saying that they had swindled Clarence out of this million-dollar business. They were alleged to have made slanderous comments about her, making her appear a criminal. She felt that was why Clarence had lost his lumber company.

The Swainstons moved to Portland, Oregon.

In the meantime, Peggy and Albert appeared together on the *Naked City* episode entitled "Button in a Haystack" as a married couple who was weathering rough times. Their characters' devotion to each other carried them through much adversity. In reality, though, the Salmis' marriage was in trouble.

Peggy had grown up feeling abandoned—with a mother who was often in jail and a father who lived apart from them—and now her husband, too, was often away working on location. Neither of the men had been rejecting her but, rather, had been forced by their careers to be elsewhere. Nevertheless, Albert's travels became a major issue, as did their disagreements about where to live.

Albert and Peggy separated in February of 1961.

He then returned to New York and was cast in *Once There Was a*

Albert and Peggy.

Russian at the Music Box Theatre on Broadway. There was a quandary in his life now: To do the work he loved to do—pure stage work, rather than watered-down screen work—put him on the opposite coast from his little daughter, and she was too young to travel alone for visits. Later, he would give up his dream and return to live in California.

In August, Peggy filed for divorce. No-fault divorce had not come into being in California yet, so she was required to place blame in order to establish grounds. The choices were adultery, extreme cruelty, willful desertion, willful neglect, habitual intemperance, conviction of a felony, or incurable insanity. None truly fit the situation, but she settled for extreme cruelty. Albert agreed that Peggy should have custody of Cas, and the couple parted amicably with a mutually-agreed settlement of $200 per month child support and $100 per month alimony.

The settlement was not enough to fully support Peggy and her daughter, so she let her agent know she was willing to go back to stage work. That would come later, but there were some television shows to do first. As a guest star on an *Untouchables* episode in 1962, she found herself working with child star Andrea Darvi. In Andrea's later book, *Pretty Babies*, she relates the atmosphere surrounding that job. Peggy, she was pleasantly surprised to learn, treated child actors with intelligence and respect. Andrea said that, in the past, such treatment had usually been reserved for adults, but Peggy was different—she had a special place in her heart for child actors. She knew that they weren't there because they necessarily wanted to be but, rather, had been put there by someone. Child actors often had adult responsibilities thrust upon them long before they were ready for it. Some were even the sole support of their parents and siblings. Peggy wanted to make Andrea's work a bit more pleasant than it would be otherwise.

While Peggy, too, had been the primary supporter of herself and her mother for many years, she also remembered so very well the good things— the wonderful roles that had been hers as a child and how well she was treated on the set by everyone concerned. Every year or two now, she would reserve some time at Twentieth Century-Fox's projection room, sit in the dark, and watch *A Tree Grows in Brooklyn* again. At such times, she couldn't help but to cry because, to her, it was so beautiful. The film itself was a lovely work of art, but it also represented to her the success and happiness of her childhood. She had been so cherished back then.

That summer, Peggy traveled in a summer stock production of *Write Me a Murder*, co-starring Mark Richman and Ethel Griffies, and directed by Christopher Hewett. Soon afterward, she did the same with *Watch the*

Albert and Peggy in a scene from *Naked City*.

Birdie. Her co-stars in this production were Alan Alda and her longtime friend Joan Blondell.

Virginia felt that Peggy was subjecting six-year-old Cas to immoral living conditions and was determined to put an end to it. Full of indignation and always with a flair for the dramatic, she sent a telegram to Peggy:

> YOUR HOUSE UNDER SURVEILLANCE SUGGEST
> YOU CONTACT YOUR LAWYER EN ROUTE WILL
> TALK TO YOU PRIOR TO CONFERENCE WITH
> JUDGE A A SCOTT OR IF PREFER YOU WANT TO
> FIGHT ME CONSULT YOUR FATHER OR YOUR AUNT
> CATHERINE WILL BE THERE THURSDAY AM DON'T
> ATTEMPT TO AVOID A MEETING I HAVE ONE CON-
> CERN THAT DARLING BABY CATHY WHERE DO YOU
> GET OFF LIVING WITH BERNSTEIN DON'T LIE
> ABOUT IT I HAVE THE FACTS

Sharing a light moment with
William Bendix.

Jerry Bernstein didn't last long in Peggy's life. Neither did her next gentleman friend. By 1964, she and Cas were living with Kenyon Foster Brown, a real estate broker, in a house at 19842 W. Grandview Drive in Topanga Canyon that he and Peggy had bought together. Virginia approved of neither Peggy's lifestyle nor Kenyon, who had told her disparaging things about Bill Garner. She felt her little granddaughter was living in an unhealthy environment and wanted to do something about it. She tried to get someone to back her up so she could rescue Cas and get Peggy some psychological help. No one was interested in participating in Virginia's cleanup campaign, so her plan fell by the wayside. It would have been quite difficult to convince Peggy to see an analyst anyway because she was very proud of the fact that, unlike many stars of the day, she had never been to one.

Nevertheless, Virginia was bound and determined to get Cas out of that house. She then came up with a plan: The child should be a ward of the court, she felt. "Albert's support [$200/month, which he was paying regularly] will take care of her school and we would take her on weekends and give her love and kindness and a respectable home." She was sure that the child support Albert was paying now was supporting Peggy's boyfriend, rather than Cas.

Little Cas' school picture. (From the collection of Jeff Howard)

There seemed to be a brick wall between Virginia and Peggy, which made helping her in any way difficult. Virginia told Bill's sister, Katherine Eckard, in a letter:

"Peggy, at 17, was fed nothing but lies about me and subjected to the vile influence of those who were advising her and today she is a shattered and broken girl. She needs help, not criticism, and to be advised in the right direction. Her father has more influence on her than anyone—therefore should tell Peggy I never got her money and relieve her of this thinking, which is where her bitterness rests where I am concerned." Later, she wrote, "She has Bill's makeup in the sense—before she would admit her guilt or wrong—she suffers. This is true with Bill as well, and is why he absorbs in alcohol for relief. Peggy's outlet has been drugs. This is now confirmed, Katherine, and she spends a minimum of $250.00 per month and it has been so stated." Virginia was sure that, had Bill demanded that Peggy move out of Hollywood and give up acting, she would have listened. "But no, he just yells and then turns around and sends money."

Virginia checked with Cas' school and had been told that they were trying to work with the child so she won't be afraid. They said she withdraws from other children, wanting to be alone, and wasn't much of a talker. This pained her grandmother. She tried to get production companies, executives, and friends to help. No one would. Virginia didn't know where else to turn.

"I knew [Cas] in Topanga in the mid-1960s when we were in the same class for a couple years at Topanga Elementary School. She was a sweet kid with really wispy white-blonde hair," says Laurie Slavin. "I remember that, for some reason, she got picked on by some of the other kids—especially the boys used to tease her—and I never knew why. She was very nice, but she probably didn't have a lot of self-confidence at that time, and kids could be cruel."

Peggy and Albert were both free to remarry in the spring of 1964. Albert soon wed a lady named Roberta Taper, and this was a marriage that would last for almost twenty-six years, the rest of his life.

Kenyon's divorce became final that spring, and, on August 6, he and Peggy took out a marriage license in New York, where she was working in summer stock. There was one error on the license: it stated that this would be Peggy's second marriage, that the marriage to Albert had been her first. Nevertheless, Peggy and Kenyon married in a civil ceremony on August 7, 1964, at the Syracuse home of Justice of the Peace Albert Gordon. Actress Joan Blondell was one of their witnesses; Jeremiah Morris of New York was the other.

Could it be mere coincidence that Peggy had starred in *A Tree Grows in Brooklyn* then married two men who hailed from Brooklyn, appeared in *Daisy Kenyon* then married a man named Kenyon? Probably so. Kenyon was a real estate man, so perhaps he would be home much more than a busy actor would. Never again would Peggy marry an actor.

CHAPTER 19

After Peggy finished her summer stock commitment at the Fayetteville Country Playhouse in New York, the newlyweds returned to Hollywood.

During this year, she did some television work—*The Man from U.N.C.L.E.* episode entitled "The Project Strigas Affair" and a guest appearance as a character named Betsy Boldface on the wildly popular *Batman* series. She appeared in one motion picture this year, entitled *The Cat*. When she wasn't acting, she was helping her husband. She had gotten her real estate license too, and was helping him sell track houses.

All was not well in paradise, however. Life with Kenyon, according to letters Cas later wrote to her grandmother, was miserable. Not only was he a violent man when he had been drinking, she wrote, but he was also into illegal activities. He was dealing in drugs and got Cas hooked on them before the age of ten. There was plenty of money as a result, and they had a five-bedroom house in Topanga, a boat, a motorcycle, four cars, and four dogs. This kind of wealth, however, came with a high emotional price tag.

Perhaps in an effort to make up for an unhappy home life, Peggy was trying to get her daughter into movies, just as her own mother had done. She wanted to give her little girl the same wonderful environment she had enjoyed each day she spent working on a film. Peggy's gentle nature was the opposite of her mother's fierce determination and aggressiveness, however, and the only movies that became available to Cas were the extremely low-budget, exploitive ones.

Virginia and Clarence were now managing a hotel. She was suffering from afar, just as much as her daughter, over Peggy's situation. It was

As Betsy Boldface on *Batman*, with Frank Gorshin.

Vacationing in Seattle. (From the collection of Jeff Howard)

obvious to her that Peggy was not in a happy marriage and that Cas was in peril. Virginia still wanted to get psychiatric help for Peggy before it was too late, but she was a barely-tolerated entity in her life these days and her well-meaning overtures were firmly rebuffed.

Peggy and eight-year-old Cas were in the car at the Pacific Coast Highway and Topanga Canyon Boulevard in Malibu one afternoon in 1965 when it crashed into a fence and flipped over. This is, apparently, a very dangerous area as the *Topanga Messenger* reported an extraordinarily high number of accidents on this boulevard. After being taken to Malibu Medical Center, Peggy was treated for a minor back injury and Cas for a bruised shoulder. The car was totaled.

Peggy was soon cast with her old friend Peter Mark Richman in the final episode of *The Outer Limits*. Filmed in 1965, this episode was entitled "The Probe." Part of the storyline involved their being afloat on a life raft during a heavy fog. "The temperature had to be reduced on the stage," says Richman. "In those days, the fog only worked in a cold atmosphere. They used to use a mineral source that would spray microscopic droplets that looked like fog and we had to breathe that stuff in. We all got very sick." He continues, "It was a terrible, terrible situation. Before each take, they would spray us with water because we were supposed to be soaking wet, and we stayed soaking wet for a week!" They came down with bronchitis, but shooting went on as scheduled. For series television, that's imperative. One cannot miss work because the show's production is on a tight schedule. "We sort of maintained some semblance of health to finish the shooting but, afterwards, we were all laid up for a couple of weeks."

That November, Peggy and Kenyon telephoned her mother. It was quite evident to Virginia that something was wrong. Peggy seemed to her to be "higher than a balloon." The Browns had just gotten back from a four-and-a-half-month trip to Mexico, they said, and had traded Cas in for a horse. Therefore, she need not worry about her granddaughter anymore. Of course, Virginia became frantic. Kenyon began cursing at her even though Peggy tried to hush him, and Virginia hung up on him.

It wasn't until she was older and more streetwise that Cas realized the purpose of the Mexican trip was probably to smuggle drugs into the country. "[Kenyon] would take me to Tijuana, Mexico, to have his Mercedes and Jaguar reupholstered with pot behind the upholstery, and our trip to Mexico was, I believe now, a big smuggling deal," she wrote Virginia many years later. Whether she was correct is unknown.

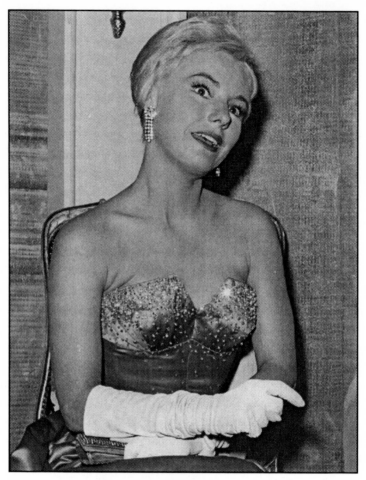

Peggy in *The Man From U.N.C.L.E.*

A few minutes after Virginia had hung up on Kenyon, Peggy called Virginia back in a more somber frame of mind to tell her that Bill Garner had died two months earlier. Now Peggy knew there would be no more chances to have her father in her life. He would always be "gone" from her. She had probably been drinking more than usual that day to help lessen the pain.

Bill's death had been sad news, but it was the danger to little Cas that frightened Virginia. Wondering how best to handle this, she wrote a letter to Kenyon's employer, Jack Linkletter, of the John Gudel Agency. She told him about the situation and begged for his help. Cas needed protection and perhaps he could provide it, she thought.

In the meantime, Virginia's husband Clarence was concerned, too. He had also been in contact with Peggy and Kenyon, and was not pleased.

He wrote a letter to Russell Eckard, whose wife, he felt, could have some influence on Peggy.

Kenyon Brown forwarded me letters my wife's mother had written and letters my wife had written Mr. Garner. These were enclosed in his letter to me. His letter advises me that by the time Peggy was 16 my wife had spent or absconded with approximately one half million dollars, Peggy's earnings. Kenyon Brown accuses my wife of swindling her own mother, of blackmailing Mr. Garner, states that she is sick, a nut and a dangerous person. And Peggy is not ashamed of anything she did or has done to her mother. That my wife is a burden and it is too bad she is not dead. As to your wife, he states she will deny that Peggy ever lived with other men, one Jerry Bernstein and one other guy, to my knowledge an Italian. As well as Kenyon Brown for over a year prior to his marriage to Peggy. However, *he* does acknowledge *he* lived with Peggy. He maintains that your wife will acknowledge nothing. If this is the case Mr. Eckerd, what was her point in confirming Mr. Garner's claims to us regard-

As a young mother in *The Cat*.

ing Peggy, and of his appealing to my wife in an effort to try and straighten her out. This was on two occasions, both at Christmastime, for two consecutive years, of which your wife has full knowledge and is fully aware.

For years Virginia has been accused of squandering Peggy's money. Well, if you or your wife would take the time and trouble to check the court records, which seemingly is what everybody fears, you would find out who got Peggy's money, one William G. H. Garner. It is these claims which have existed over a period of years and which your wife has been a party to that has destroyed the lives of several people. And since my marriage to Virginia basically caused me to lose a million dollar business. And for which I have filed a million dollar suit for recovery. This is attributed to reports that are known to consistently come from Peggy about her mother. Virginia attributes this not to Peggy on any willful part of hers, but from the time the girl was 16 years old she was led to believe that her mother got her money, or that it was used to pay bills etc., on Virginia's behalf. Well, Mr. Eckerd, this is just not so. And I have the fraudulent accounting to the court that Mr. Garner gave, as well as his fraudulent Petitions that made it possible that a guardianship was turned over to him. And you, Mr. Eckerd or Peggy can never refute this.

Mr. Garner had to paint Virginia black to his own daughter, as well as one Edward D. Dibs, to accomplish any cooperation from Peggy that might have existed in getting this guardianship transferred. He even lied about letters of Peggy's that were on file; attached herewith you find a court record to the contrary. Then when they sent Peggy out of the state without Virginia's approval, he was in more serious trouble than his perjury to the court. I trust you are aware they sent a minor across a state line without the approval of the parent who held her legal custody, never mind any guardianship, and withheld her whereabouts for intervals of five to ten days at a time from her mother. They were guilty of kidnapping. Moreover, the fact that she was sent out of the state for the purpose of entering into fraudulent business negotiations where her earnings were concerned were even more serious. All of these things Mr. Garner knew, and was the reason he sat on a barstool and for years had nothing but a whiskey soaked brain. Either you or Mrs. Eckerd need only to check this man's Army record, as well as his record with the Government and I assure you, you will find it anything but honorable. But this was all to be suppressed and Virginia was an easy target for those involved to blame.

Later in the letter, he continued,

> Mr. Eckerd, I would like you to know that Kenyon Brown is the man that told me Mr. Garner was a no good so and so, and just a drunken slob, and etc. He also told me he did not want to marry Peggy, and that he liked little Kathy, but not enough that he could love her. He stated Peggy never took care of her, and on one occasion he stated he was going to throw her over a cliff. And very recently, when they called to inform us of Mr. Garner's death they were going to trade her in on a horse.
>
> Mr. Garner informed me the amount of money Peggy spent on pills, which was $400 a month, and on one occasion he told me she had a drug bill in the amount of $1400. Kenyon Brown informed me Peggy was spending that amount on pills and he had cut her down to $250 per month. I might also tell you I can bring in friends of Peggy's who will confirm Kenyon Brown has made these statements.
>
> Peggy had asked us for money two consecutive years, both occasions were times when Mr. Garner had first called us. Peggy had told us she was stone broke, she needed clothes to go to New York to do a show, etc., and I forwarded her money and paid for the clothes…A year ago when my financial status became such, over losing my business, I asked Peggy and Kenyon Brown to reimburse me. Kenyon Brown assured me he would pay this, but of course, he never has.

Further, it said,

> I want you to also be advised that Kenyon Brown's letter states that Virginia's suing the state is laughable and for 20 years she has been fighting a lost cause. This later statement practi-

cally insures the fact that Peggy has been the person to peddle this kind of stuff and she has not only done it with Kenyon Brown, but she did it with two other husbands as well. And I think it is high time that this young lady be turned around on a dime and be exposed.

The letter concludes with an ultimatum:

> I think she [Eckard's wife, Peggy's Aunt Catherine] should tell Peggy to make certain to write to her mother and give her the facts and details of her father's death and cease this JUNK and lies she has been peddling for years. Or she can inform Peggy I will personally file a Petition that will bring both Peggy and Kenyon Brown into court and clear her mother, and we will let the chips fall where they will.

(It seems that either Virginia's and Clarence's letter-writing styles were amazingly similar or Virginia might have written this letter, then presented it to Clarence for his signature. In any event, they would later learn that the Browns' trading Cas in for a horse was, of course, just a joke. There's no way Peggy would have let that really happen.)

Virginia just couldn't let go of the past and was practically making herself sick over all the injustices she felt that she and Peggy had experienced in life. The world must be made aware, she felt, of what a cruelly destructive environment the entertainment industry was—how they used and manipulated people, ruining their lives, in order to line their own pockets—and she wanted the perpetrators put in jail. She wrote to a man whose judgment she respected, and asked him what he thought of the idea of her filing for divorce so that she would have the opportunity to tell the divorce court all about the miseries she and Peggy have had to endure all these years. She hoped that the court session would have heavy media coverage and the villains in her life would be publicly exposed.

Judge A. A. Scott, Judge of the Superior Court in Los Angeles and the very embodiment of common sense, responded by trying to calm her down. He advised her to refrain from corresponding with Peggy in any way. "You have enough problems of your own in taking care of your good husband, without worrying yourself sick about Peggy," he said. He sympathized with Virginia's long-suffering husband, telling her, "Your present husband has been very good to you. He has suffered a great deal, not only by embarrassment, but unnecessary harassment from those who are still hounding you, so live for him, Virginia, and forget the past. Start life anew up there in Portland, and let bygones be bygones." As for the divorce idea, he felt it was ludicrous and expressed a great deal of frustration in his advice. "Frankly, I am at a loss to understand why you are even thinking of starting a divorce suit for the mere purpose of airing out your whole life in a divorce court. You can gain absolutely nothing by it, and certainly Clarence's case, as far as the Big Bear litigation is concerned, will not be helped at all. So forget all about such nonsense. You say in one breath that you are happily married to Clarence. For God's sake stay that way, and forget everybody else."

It's not because her mother accepted defeat gracefully that Peggy had starred in movies. Rather, it was Virginia's strong-willed determination that had gotten her there, and that's what kept Virginia from giving up on her cause now. She continued to write letters about the injustices to friends and politicians on all levels. Something, she felt, simply *must* be done about the deplorable situation. Otherwise, the industry will continue its evil ways and people will continue to be victimized by it. Almost inevitably, the politicians' response was that they could do nothing to help her. She had written frequent and very long, detailed letters to them, pleading for their help, following up with numerous phone calls, but she seems to have been regarded as simply a pest. Perhaps they were overwhelmed by the extreme length and complexity of her pleadings, not to mention the social and political power of the people she claimed were the guilty parties. Most of the politicians gave her a polite brush-off.

Virginia's letters to Peggy, too, could have used a psychologist's guidance. They were also very, very long and often had a nagging, self-righteous quality to them. Instead of bringing them together as she intended, they were driving her daughter further away.

Peggy's life, like her mother's, seems to have now been at its lowest point.

While at the Fernwood Market in Topanga Canyon to buy meat one day, Peggy met a young man named Ed Jenkins. While he was highly intelligent in the area of science, he was going through a hippie phase and had not fully developed his social skills. Her heart went out to this man, and she offered him a job—helping her around the house and driving her to her appointments or errands in her Jaguar XJ-120. When Kenyon had her Jaguar, they would use the Mercedes. Ed jumped at the chance, and so began a very meaningful relationship that changed his life. There was about a twelve-year difference in their ages, but the two got along quite well.

Ed would walk the mile to Peggy's house each day and arrive as she and her family were finishing breakfast. Cas would be dressed and ready to go to school while Kenyon would be sitting at the kitchen table, reading the newspaper. The man's outgoing, optimistic nature made him seem larger than life to Ed. Peggy would cheerfully offer Ed a cup of coffee. Ed or Peggy would soon take Cas to the lumber store where the bus would pick her up for school, and then Ed would drive Peggy wherever she needed to go. As soon as they left the house, Peggy's beautiful smile would vanish. "Not always to sadness or melancholy," Ed says, "but up and down during the day." Most of the time, they went shopping or to the movies. Her Academy card allowed her free admission to most films. He also took her to the Spann Ranch in Santa Susana Canyon where her horse was stabled. When they weren't out and about, they spent many happy hours in the Browns' above-ground swimming pool. It soon became apparent that Peggy was lonely, and what she needed most was someone in whom she could confide. Ed willingly supplied that sympathetic ear whenever the need arose.

It surprised him that Kenyon seemed almost secondary in her life, as if he were merely an afterthought. He was very much on both of their minds one day, however: Peggy had lent Ed her Jaguar and he had been cruising Hollywood in it with a friend on a rainy day. They hit a slick spot in the road and the car slid, hitting another car. When he ruefully confessed to Peggy what had occurred, they became very worried that Kenyon would find out and fire him. Peggy knew of a body shop in Beverly Hills that would take care of it, and it was fixed without Kenyon ever knowing.

Very soon, the relationship between Ed and Peggy took on another dimension. Peggy enjoyed reenacting for him scenes of her past projects. In the pool one day, she and Ed were alone. She was at the other side of the pool from him and began singing "That Old Black Magic," the song her Cherie character had sung in the play *Bus Stop*, while her leading man, Albert Salmi, had looked on admiringly. As the song and dialog progressed, she seemed to become another person—Cherie. She inched her way through the pool toward Ed until she ended her song by tenderly kissing him. "Perhaps this was reliving some time in her past with Albert?" Ed wonders. "Could I have been a substitute for him?"

Ed might be right. Just like Albert, he was 6'2", had light hair and was quiet-natured.

Peggy and Ed then became lovers. "Peggy was a very warm and tender lover," he recalls, "and showed me how to be involved with a woman during lovemaking." Just as he was filling a need in her life, she was also helping Ed a great deal. She was a very giving, caring person—exactly what he needed then.

They later went together to the Bluegrass Festival at the Topanga campground by the river and the strawberry festival at the Topanga Grange. Sometimes, they would just spend time looking out at the ocean together.

"She referred to Albert as 'Daniel Boone' [the television series in which, during its first season, Albert was a regular]," Ed recalls. "She had me drive her by his house several times and became very sad and sullen." Could it be that Peggy regretted divorcing Albert? Was her marriage to Kenyon not what she expected, and was she wishing she could have Albert back? Even though he loved New York, he was still living in California; and he had a television series now that filmed in this area, so he wasn't traveling all the time. The life Albert was living now could have been hers if she had stayed with him. If she had only waited.

"Never saw her what I would consider drunk but a little high, yes. She would almost always have a drink when we were in the pool and, after one or two, would do the 'Black Magic' thing."

Peggy and Ed had many happy times together. She introduced him to elegant dining. Her favorite restaurants were Chez Jay's in Santa Monica and Chez Voltaire in Beverly Hills. Peggy would be dressed beautifully at these times, and she bought Ed some nice clothes for such occasions too.

When Ed's mother and stepfather came to visit him, Peggy bought food, delivered it to his place, and cooked a wonderful meal for them. Once it was ready, she left so he and his family could enjoy their dinner in private. His mother remembers Peggy as charming and very gracious.

All good things must end, though. After about a year, it became necessary for Ed to move away. In looking back now at those days he spent with Peggy, thoughts of her give him a general feeling of goodness. She was such a good, caring person. "She taught me to value myself and gave me confidence with women," he says. He would never forget her.

By the next year, Peggy's unhappy marriage seems to have taken its toll. The May 1966 edition of *Movie Life* ran an article entitled "Yesterday's Stars." The current photos of the other stars were much more flattering than hers. Peggy appeared bedraggled and sad. She had no makeup on. Her straight, blonde hair's dark roots were very evident. It appeared she had been crying. Did they just catch her at a bad time, or was that indicative of her life at that point?

Peggy and Kenyon's marriage might not have given her the love she craved, but it did provide her with financial stability. That fall, she bought some property of her own. Her mailing address was now in Malibu.

In February of 1967, Virginia received a letter from her deceased ex-husband's life insurance company, informing her that she was entitled to half of the twelve-thousand-dollar value of the policy, even though she was no longer married to him. That money would certainly come in handy!

Peggy had been pregnant again but lost the baby, and was now starting to wonder if she, too, would become a casualty of this marriage. According to a letter Cas wrote to her grandmother, Kenyon had endangered Peggy's life multiple times. Once, he threw a small television set at her head but, just in the nick of time, Cas pushed her mother out of harm's way. That night, Kenyon threw Cas off a second-story porch and made her sleep outside. "It was terrible and very scary and something I'll *never forget*," she wrote. "I could still hear arguments inside, just praying everything would be okay the next day. I was too afraid to go back inside because when Kenyon got drunk, he was a totally different and scary person."

Another time, Kenyon ran after Peggy with a fireplace poker. Cas, again, tried to protect her mother and ended up being smacked in the nose and face, then thrown onto the pavement. Once, Peggy was getting into their car and had only her foot inside when Kenyon slammed the door and dragged her alongside the car.

The soft gentleness that had been so much a part of who Peggy was was not as evident now. She had developed a protective shell around herself. Peggy couldn't take Kenyon's abuse any longer and filed for divorce. Ending in 1969, their marriage had lasted five years.

When they parted ways, Kenyon took the two good cars, leaving Peggy the two that didn't work. She had to have reliable transportation, though, so she placed a call to her friend Barbara Whiting Smith, whose husband was general director of advertising for General Motors. The Whitings arranged a good deal for her, and she went to the Pontiac dealership in Santa Monica to sign the papers.

Now Peggy had to earn a living. How she yearned for good, quality roles. Acting is what she did best. The talent was still there. Why couldn't casting directors see that? It just wasn't Peggy's nature to go out and drum up business for herself, however. In the past, it was her mother and agents who did that. Because of her fear of rejection, it took a major effort on her part to contact people to let them know she was available for film work. She got out and did it, though, leaving Cas alone in the house a good deal of the time.

Albert had visitation rights, so his wife, Roberta, and their daughter, Lizanne, went to pick the child up for one of her visits to the Salmi home. While there, Roberta looked through Peggy's cupboards and refrigerator,

With Charlton Heston in *The Hallmark Hall of Fame.*

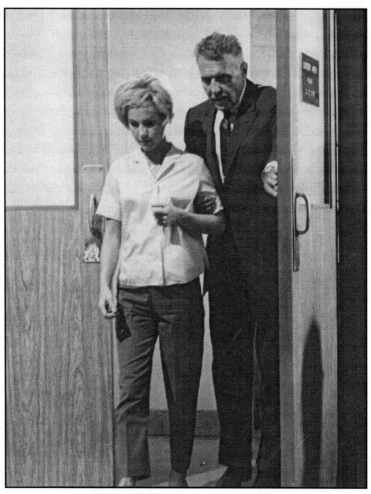

With Ralph Bellamy in *Alcoa Premiere*.

finding nothing there but alcohol. She reported the condition of Peggy's house to Albert, and he decided to take action. That was no environment for a child, so, with Peggy's approval, he asked the Court for and received custody of Cas in 1970.

Cas was thirteen years old when she went to live in her father's house. At first, she was quite happy there and enjoyed getting to know her two little half-sisters better and spending more time with her father. One of Albert's hobbies was playing cards, so he taught Cas how to play some games. She treasured those times in the den, playing cards with her daddy.

In mid-December, the Salmis received a letter and check from Virginia:

Dear Albert and Roberta.

It was nice talking to you and thank you for your kindness and courtesy. Albert, you will never know how relieved I am, knowing you have Cas. I know she is much better off with you and I'm sure she must be much happier.

If my friend Judge Scott was the judge who gave you custody, I wanted to thank him. I had called on him on more than one occasion. My brother, who has been out here twice since July to help me get Clarence's estate settled, also is relieved to know Cas is with you.

This a.m. I received Cas' Xmas card and you can be sure I shed tears of joy. This is the first Xmas or anything I ever had a card from her. She is my only grandchild, Albert, and you will never know the heartaches. I had been denied a chance to really be around her or to get her to know me as I am, not as she was led to believe. How I'd love to bake her cookies, etc., over the years, but I never had a chance. She was so pretty the last time I saw her for such a few moments.

I called Peggy, but as usual she has her same attitude. I will get her a nightgown, which she asked for Xmas, and I hope the future will be different. Enclosed is a cashier's check for which I ask you to please get something for Cas from me. I'm sure Roberta will know what she would like or need. Also enclosed is a card for the package. Really wanted to send more but, with my phone calls plus dental experience, this was all my budget will stand.

Thank you again and have a very merry Xmas.

Grandma Virginia Garner Swainston

The Salmis had one Christmas tradition that must have seemed strange to Cas. According to a neighbor, the family wasn't allowed to bring out the yuletide decorations until the visit from Roberta's brother was over. Devoutly Jewish, he never did approve of his sister having married a Christian. Once he was gone, though, the Christmas decorations went up and the family enjoyed the joyous season. On the night of Christmas Eve, the children would leave cookies and milk out for Santa, then go to bed. The next morning, the girls found not only gifts galore under the tree,

Cas with her little half sisters, Jenny and Lizanne Salmi.
(From the Salmi family collection)

but also proof positive that it was Santa who put them there: shoe prints leading from the fireplace to the tree and back. Only the most observant person would notice that the tracks that were left exactly matched the size of Albert's shoes. He was happy to do his part to make this a joyous day for the youngsters.

Chapter 20

Acting jobs were slow in coming, so Peggy earned a living as a real estate broker. Using her maiden name, Peggy sold houses for William Justice Company in Brentwood.

Arthur Jacobson had been Peggy's friend for many years and now saw how difficult it was for her to support herself in California, where the cost of living was so high. A recent widower, he opened his Pacific Palisades home to her, and she gratefully moved in. He had faith in her and gave her the emotional support she so desperately needed.

Peggy had always had a fondness for older men, and Artie had known her since the golden years of her youth when he was assistant director of two of her films, *Junior Miss* and *Thunder in the Valley*. Three decades her senior, he was a father figure to Peggy and, for the rest of her life, would be there for her as her real father had not been.

Conversely, Virginia was now alone. Her husband, Clarence, had died in August 1969, a year after they had established an organization called Journey for Justice. Virginia had overdrawn the company bank account so much that the bank had asked her to close it. Things were not looking good for her.

Peggy started receiving puzzling telephone calls from Albert's wife, Roberta, who would call to harass her with filthy language, then leave her receiver off the hook so Peggy would not be able to make any outgoing calls. So upsetting were these calls that, when Peggy had been drinking heavily, she would sometimes have hallucinations that Roberta's face was on the ceiling, on the lampshade, on the walls, everywhere. What she might not have realized was that this same woman was also being physically and emotionally abusive to Cas.

191

Another beautiful portrait by Roddie McDowall.
(Used with permission from Virginia McDowall)

From the time the child had moved into their home, Roberta had made it clear to Cas that she was unwelcome. She hated her, she said, for being Albert's firstborn. She wanted her own child to have that distinction. Cas, a very sensitive girl, was hurt to the quick. When Albert was away working on location, Roberta was cruelly punitive—beating Cas and her own youngest daughter, Jenny, on the back with a belt, or making Cas eat a snail out of the garden as penance for some misdeed. Once, Cas got a C on an English test, which didn't suit Roberta at all, so she humiliated the child by cutting her hair off. Another time, both Cas and Jenny were locked out of the house at night with only one blanket to keep them warm. It was painful for Cas to see little Jenny being sent outside with a sign on her back saying she was for sale, or dropped off in a strange neighborhood because her mother said she wasn't loved or wanted anymore. "She drug us by the hair a lot and hit us a lot and blamed everything Lizanne did [on us]."

Such treatment was taking a heavy toll on Cas, who found herself wishing out loud that she were dead. Roberta responded to that by daring her to drink a bottle of rubbing alcohol. Cas picked up the bottle and did, indeed, begin drinking from it. Roberta, her bluff having been called in front of a witness (Cas' school friend), quickly got an antidote and administered it to the child.

In February of 1971, Virginia got a very strange card from her granddaughter. It said, "Dear Granda [sic]—Please try to committ [sic] my mom for me. Have a very happy Valentines day. Next Tuesday, I'll send the flowers to you. Don't be to [sic] upset, Because of my Mother. I hope you like this card. I hope I can see you sometime. I'm so glad that I'm not living with my mother anymore. Tell me if you get this on Valentines Day."

Later, when Virginia mentioned this note to her, Cas had no memory of having written it or that she had ever wanted Peggy to be committed. She loved her mother and her mother loved her. The handwriting was very similar to Cas', however, so she did apparently write it, but it might have been during a time she was under the influence of drugs. Since being introduced to them by Kenyon a few years earlier, she had not been able to break free of the addiction.

Albert's wife urged Virginia to come to California to help commit Peggy to a mental hospital. She had brain damage, Roberta said, and was doing very strange things, not the least of which was robbery. Virginia consulted with a detective by the name of Greco. After checking into the matter, he reported that only part of what Roberta had said might have been true, but the rest was not. Virginia knew that robbery would be very much out of character for Peggy, and she now was starting to doubt Roberta's integrity.

"I do not believe it is beyond the realm of possibility," Virginia wrote to a friend, when they suspected the mental instability was Roberta's, rather than Peggy's. "Jealousy could be a factor here where Roberta Salmi is concerned and her very serious allegations. She openly stated she doesn't like Peggy and I fear this could be a means to hurt her more."

It was Peggy's nature to just carry on with her life in spite of obstacles in her path. Even though she wasn't cast in films much anymore, she was far from forgotten by her fans. In the summer of 1971, the annual *Screen Greats* magazine came out. This edition was entitled "Hollywood Nostalgia" and spotlighted the stars of yesteryear who they considered to have been the greatest. Peggy was included in the Kids section, along with some of her early co-stars—Roddy McDowall, Margaret O'Brien and Elizabeth Taylor. The article about them was focused on the premise that they don't make child stars the way they did back in the 1930s and 1940s. It concluded, "No, there are no child stars today who can really compare with those of the past. Not in the movies—not even on television where most of them have taken refuge. So raise high your glasses—your Shirley Temple milk glasses, of course—and drink one last cup to days—and kids—gone by. You will not see their like again."

Back in Brentwood, Cas couldn't take Roberta's abuse anymore, so at age fourteen she ran away with nothing more than the clothes on her back. She went to McClaren Hall, a shelter for abused children. At first, she was afraid to go back to the Salmi house, but she was eventually persuaded to return. When she did, she discovered that Roberta had burned all the things that were precious to her—her creative writings, school albums, record albums, even her clothes. Cas had written some TV scripts that Albert was going to submit for her, but Roberta got to them first and burned them, too.

Since Cas was back and had only one outfit, Roberta had no choice but to buy her more clothes. Once Albert was away on location again, however, the abuse at home resumed. Cas became even more frightened of her stepmother when she discovered books about black magic among her things.

Then Cas' paternal grandmother came to live with them, and it seemed that things were finally starting to look up. Ida Salmi was a sweet lady, a native of Finland, but her English was not very good. Albert was able to converse with his mother in Finnish, however, and the two were very close.

One day, Cas and the housekeeper were left alone with Ida. It was midday, so they took lunch out to the backyard where Ida was sitting in the lounge chair. She didn't move. Something was wrong, so they thought the best way to handle that was to get Ida into the house where she could be near a phone. They carried her inside and Cas called her dad at the studio, hoping that he could talk to Ida in Finnish and find out what the problem was. She was still unresponsive, however. Albert said he'd be right home. In the meantime, they called the paramedics, who were there when he arrived. The ambulance took Ida to Cedars of Lebanon Hospital, where she was diagnosed as having suffered a cerebral hemorrhage. She died three days later.

Albert was absolutely devastated. He silently grieved for weeks. Cas was to blame for Ida's death, Roberta told him. If she hadn't carried her into the house, his mother would not have died. The very thought sickened Albert. Rather than say destructive things to Cas, he didn't speak to her at all for two weeks, withdrawing into himself instead.

Roberta gave Cas a severe beating in punishment.

Having now lost her grandmother and feeling that she no longer had the emotional support of her father, Cas felt very much alone at the Salmi house. She ran away for good at the age of fifteen. She lived on the streets for a while, using the Salmis' drugstore credit to buy the supplies she needed. Once caught for doing that, she escaped from her captor, then went back to live with her mother at Artie Jacobson's apartment.

Cas tried to take Roberta to court for child abuse. Perhaps that would help Jenny. Even though she got documentation from neighbors and the school nurse, her efforts proved unsuccessful. Cas felt that the Salmis' money and status had undermined the case. In retaliation, Roberta tried to have Cas committed to Camarillo State Hospital, but she, too, was unsuccessful.

It is said that a mistreated child should tell a trusted adult about any abuse she receives. Cas did that many times, but it helped not one bit. The system had failed her. She was a survivor by nature, however. She wished she could rescue Jenny and their father from the ugliness, but saw no way that that would be possible.

CHAPTER 21

Life at her mother's home might have been neglectful, but at least it wasn't overtly abusive anymore now that Kenyon was gone. The worst that would happen these days was that she might be locked out of the apartment for staying out past her curfew. She could handle that. She would just sleep out in the hallway, where it was warm.

Peggy had left the real estate profession and become a fleet sales manager at the same Pontiac dealership in Santa Monica from which she had bought a car a few years earlier. Later, she would get a similar job but with a higher salary as the first saleswoman at Speight Buick-Opel on Santa Monica Boulevard in Hollywood.

"It's not all that different from acting," she told UPI writer Vernon Scott. "You try to be honest and sincere. You have to sell yourself before you sell anything else. That's how it is playing a character for a film or TV."

"Remember Peggy Ann Garner, who won a special Oscar for her portrayal of Francie in *A Tree Grows in Brooklyn?*" asked the *L.A. Harold Examiner*. "She is now the first feminine sales representative ever hired for Speight Buick in Hollywood. Peggy, always an underplayer, promises a soft sell on the new models."

On the ads this dealership ran was the phrase "Where the stars buy their cars" and photos of Betty Mann (PR & Sales) and Peggy Ann Garner (Sales). This is where Peggy was working when her daughter came back to live with her. After a while, a Chevrolet dealership offered Peggy a fleet-managerial position at an even higher salary, so she accepted that. Peggy had always liked cars, so she now felt she was doing something in the "real world" that was actually interesting. She was working on a commission basis five and a half days a week, and doing rather well. She and her employer had a deal—if a good television or film role was offered, Peggy could take time off to do it. This seemed like the best of both worlds, and it was always fun when customers would ask for her autograph after learning who she was. She would occasionally show up on television, too, in her employer's commercials.

Now, as always, Peggy would have been the peppy, enthusiastic one on the set and would do a wonderful job—but the offers just weren't coming. She was having a prolonged dry spell in both television shows and films. She would sometimes go for interviews at the studios, but was turned down again and again. "They didn't give me a chance," she'd tell Artie. "They didn't even know I had once won an Oscar. They treated me like dirt." She would then break down in tears.

Even so, Peggy *was* still being interviewed by reporters now and then. They were often interested in doing "Where are they now?" stories of former child stars and seemed fascinated by the fact that Peggy had to make her living elsewhere, rather than by acting. Not happy with her natural light brown hair, she was now presenting herself to the world with whitish-blonde hair. Members of the press weren't sure if it was real or a wig. Whatever it was, it didn't look natural, they said.

At forty years of age, though, Peggy was still as perky as ever when *Candid Press* interviewed her in 1972. If the reporter brought up a negative topic, such as the whereabouts of all the money she had earned as a child, Peggy would wrap that subject up as quickly and diplomatically as possible. It had been all gone for years, she admitted, but she did not wish to discuss it further. Introducing a new topic, Peggy said that she was fortunate that beauty was never a part of her image. She felt she had much less to lose by aging than the glamorous stars did. Indeed, Hollywood is not a good town for an aging movie star, especially a female one.

Reporter Dora Albert had first interviewed Peggy in the mid-1940s, and had the happy assignment of checking back with her now to see how she was faring. Ms. Albert was struck by how beautiful she was—"At 40," she wrote in the May 1973 issue of *Modern Screen*, "she looks young for her age. Her figure is slim; her green eyes sparkle and her skin is as soft as that of a girl of 17. Her blonde hair was swept up, and she was wearing a smart black dress with a white collar and cuffs."

"I wouldn't trade my life for anything in the world," Peggy told reporters with a smile. She tried to always look on the bright side, especially with the press. She suffered much, however. The elements of her life to which the press wasn't privy included Peggy's dependence on narcotics and alcohol, her past struggle for survival, and her love-hate feelings toward her mother. It seems the only way she could get along with Virginia was from a distance. Peggy did not enjoy being with her, but would try to make up for it by sending her upbeat cards. Letters to her mother were much less frequent, but were, also, filled with forced cheerfulness.

When Cas walked through the room during one particular interview, the reporter noticed how much she looked like her father. She was tall with a light complexion and naturally-blonde hair. She had inherited not only Albert's physical qualities, but also his artistic creativity; she loved to paint pictures and designs. Like her mother, she also enjoyed writing poetry and stories. The genes for creative talent had come at Cas from all directions and, if it would be nurtured and developed, she could achieve a great deal of success in life.

Cas' childhood friend, Laurie Slavin, was working now at Fernood Market in Topanga after school, so Cas would drop by regularly to see her. "She had blossomed into quite a young beauty," Laurie says. "I was so happy for her because she really looked beautiful then with a very nice, trim figure."

Peggy was telling reporters that Cas wanted to be a movie star, but she was urging her to choose another occupation—*any* other occupation. Her daughter had been through hell, through no fault of her own. All Peggy wished for her was as carefree an adolescence as possible.

It was not to be. Cas quit school after tenth grade, became pregnant and had a baby girl in 1973, when she was only sixteen. She knew she couldn't give this tiny child the kind of life she deserved, so she gave her baby up for adoption. The following year, she married her daughter's father, nineteen-year-old Scott Franklin Clark. Finding marriage not what they thought it would be, they soon went their separate ways, but apparently never officially divorced.

In the meantime, Virginia was carving out a niche for herself in Portland. Every November since 1971, she and her friend Iola Williamson would begin work on their "dollies." In cooperation with the Portland Fire Department's Toy and Joy Makers program, they would make dozens of little outfits, dressing the many dolls that would be distributed to needy little girls at Christmastime. It gave Virginia a profound sense of accomplishment and pleasure to donate her time and talents for this worthy project, and the resulting publicity did much to boost her self-esteem.

During the weeks between Thanksgiving and Christmas, when most people were in a joyful holiday spirit, Virginia sent this confrontational telegram to Albert Salmi:

DEAR ALBERT I WANT IMMEDIATE CONFIRMATION FROM YOUR WIFE ROBERTA AS TO HER CLAIMS SHE BELIEVE PEGGY ANN GARNER HAD BRAIN DAMAGE AND WAS BEYOND HELP. I WANT TO FURTHER CONFIRM THAT YOUR DAUGHTER CATHERINE CONFIRMS HER REQUEST TO ME HER GRAND-MOTHER I HAVE HER MOTHER PEGGY ANN GAR-NER COMMITTED TO A MENTAL HOSPITAL...ALSO I WANT ESTABLISHED THE DATE THE BIRTH OF CATHERINE'S CHILD WHETHER OR NOT SHE WAS MARRIED OTHERWISE LETS HAVE A PRESS CONFER-ENCE AND THROW THIS WIDE OPEN.

VIRGINIA

It's not known whether Albert knew about the source of these allegations, but to respond with the truth would have made both of his wives look bad. He was more afraid of Roberta than he was of Virginia, though, so he chose to ignore the telegram.

Oblivious to the latest of her mother's issues, Peggy now had a canine "man" in her life—a little Yorkshire terrier named Jake. She just adored this tiny dog, and he was a faithful companion for her.

"There is something about [Peggy] that is as sturdy as an oak tree," Dora Albert had written in a 1973 issue of *Modern Screen*. "You feel that she can bend with the wind but she will never break."

The casting director of the daytime drama *General Hospital* was a longtime friend of Peggy's. Through this connection, she was given a role on that show and was soon offered a one-year contract as a regular. Even though she loved acting and needed the money, she was hesitant. It would require moving to New York, and she didn't know how such a move would affect her beloved Jake. She turned it down.

In 1977 the bottom had dropped out of the car business, so Peggy was hoping to get back into acting there on the west coast. When she discovered that a segment of a *Police Woman* episode was being filmed right outside her apartment building, she went outside to watch. She spotted Angie Dickinson and Earl Holliman, and told them that she was interested in acting again, asking them to put in a good word for her with their casting director. They were happy to do so, and Peggy was invited to play the part of a probation officer on the series. It was only for one episode but it might lead to bigger things.

That day in front of her apartment was the first time that Earl Holliman had ever seen Peggy in person, but he was already an admirer from years back. He says, "I, too, was a huge fan of Peggy Ann Garner, starting with *A Tree Grows in Brooklyn*. Sadly, we were only acquaintances." He recalls her as a very sweet person, and was pleased that he could help her get that job.

Even though it was difficult for Peggy to ask people for work, she did it anyway. She called some of her old friends; William Dozier, retired head of Screen Gems, got his daughter Debbie, of the Bret Adams Agency, to act as Peggy's agent. "It's funny, her being my agent," Peggy said, "because I used to hold her in my arms when she was a baby." Debbie got right to work and soon things began to happen. It was announced in the newspapers that Peggy had signed to play the studio teacher in the Ten-Four Productions' NBC special about Judy Garland entitled *Rainbow*. That's a role she could easily play, having been taught in the studio school herself as a child. Something went wrong, though. Even on the DVD of this movie, Peggy wasn't there. In fact, there was no scene at all involving a studio teacher. It appears that her scenes had ended up on the cutting room floor. The director of that film? Jackie Cooper.

Things soon got better, though. Peggy was given a part in the 1978 film *A Wedding* that brought together many big names in the business. The director was her friend Robert Altman.

Lee Graham of the *Canyon Crier* heralded Peggy's appearance in this film: "Peggy Ann Garner, who has been working for General Motors as a fleet car executive, is returning to the screen. Robert Altman cast the former child star in *A Wedding*, which is filming in Lake Bluff, Illinois. Incidentally, Peggy Ann recently became a grandmother. Feel older?"

Carol Burnett, who had a major role in this film, states, "Ms. Garner was terrific to work with. The cast all got along very well." She felt that they were "one big, happy gang."

Dina Merrill, who also co-starred in this film, agrees that "she was very happy to be there with all of us." Peggy's work habits were impeccable, she says. "She was always well prepared and very professional in

With Carol Burnett in *A Wedding.*

every phase of her work." Dina enjoyed being with her, saying, "She got along beautifully with all of us. She was cheerful and pleasant to be with—and above all, a good actress!"

Between scenes, Peggy could sometimes be found sitting on the sidelines, wearing her glasses, busily knitting.

During this year she also appeared in a made-for-television movie entitled *Betrayal.* As a result, a letter appeared in a television question-and-answer column, asking if that woman could possibly be the same Peggy Ann Garner who had played the sweet little Francie in *A Tree Grows in Brooklyn* thirty-three years earlier. People sometimes had a hard time accepting the fact that their dear, adorable Peggy Ann had grown up.

Virginia's sentiments exactly. Back in Oregon, she reminisced fondly of the happy times she and her daughter had had long ago and sometimes wistfully dreamed of what could have been, but felt that the film industry had selfishly manipulated both her and Peggy to the detriment of both. Nevertheless, there was happiness in her life these days. She had reestablished communication with Cas while the child was living at the Salmis' home, and warm, supportive letters flowed back and forth between them. Life without Clarence was lonely, and a letter from Cas was the bright spot in many a day. Visits from her granddaughter lit up her life.

Back to a favorite hobby between scenes.

Unlike her grandmother, Cas wasn't prone to dwell on wrongs done to her in the past. Instead, she was making her way in the world as best she could. She had never seen what a good, healthy marriage looked like up close, but both of her parents *did* set a good example when it came to work habits. She showed the same strong work ethic throughout the ensuing years and took jobs that almost inevitably involved serving others. Cas worked as waitress-hostess, took care of a sick woman, tended bar, served as receptionist, and cleaned houses. She was good at earning money, but not at spending it wisely. Cas had a soft heart and would often lend money to people who didn't pay her back, or she would use it to buy alcohol or drugs to satisfy her own addictions. When she was in an environment in which she would be so tempted, she would gamble. As a result, money problems were ever present in her life. It might have been because of visits by creditors that she would sometimes move suddenly without leaving a forwarding address. By December 1978, Cas had moved to Salem, Oregon to be closer to her grandmother.

Virginia urged Cas to face up to her problems. Running away from them, she said, would only serve to make them worse. Nevertheless, she sympathized with her granddaughter, feeling that her childhood had been a tragic one ever since the age of four, when her parents split up. Virginia did what she could to make up for that.

Sometimes, it seemed to Cas that Grandma was the only person in the world who loved her. At Virginia's prompting, she confided in her about the extent of the abuse she and her half-sister had received from Roberta and the fact that Roberta had tried to shoot Albert at least once.

Virginia was a woman of action and wanted to help. She sent a mailgram to Albert and Roberta, confronting them about these things. She asked him why he didn't report his wife to the police, and continued, "Now Albert, I have been through hell and I don't have to take anything from anybody anymore, but I want to know if your wife Roberta is completely nuts when she sends her children out with signs on their backs that they're for sale. Without any delay whatsoever I want to talk to your agent or you get your butt up here to Portland where your lovely daughter is."

Albert did not want to believe such terrible things about Roberta. Yes, he knew she was abusive to him, but surely she wouldn't do those things to a child. Ever loyal, he would come to Roberta's defense whenever people would criticize her. In this case, Albert would rather avoid the situation entirely than to find himself in the middle of a confrontation between two such strong-willed women as Virginia and Roberta. To do otherwise would have been a no-win situation.

Cas enjoyed being with her grandmother, but moved back to California in September 1979. Through good times and bad times, though, Cas always kept the faith. Sometimes, others helped her in that effort. Writing to her grandmother, she said, "Kia, the lady I was taking care of, passed away about 2 weeks ago. I was relieved because I knew she wouldn't suffer anymore and is free and in peace. She really prepared me for her ascension and freedom. It was hard at first, but I'm starting to accept it."

In the meantime, Peggy was invited to be a presenter for the first annual Youth in Film Awards on October 14, 1979. This is where she met former child star Sybil Jason, who was co-hosting the event with Jackie Coogan. "We arranged for ex-child stars to present the new child stars with their awards," says Sybil. "Peg was one of them and, from the very first moment of introduction, we felt like we had known each other for years.

"After the award show was over, we became extremely close. My husband and I had turned our three-car garage into a little theater where we viewed the movies that our friends had starred in, and it had a delightful little stage where we could do improvs or anything else we wanted to 'try out.' It was always a lot of fun and Peggy fell so much in love with our little theater that she seriously wanted to move into it and live there!"

Sybil continues, "One of the biggest compliments I have personally felt proud of was after I had appeared on television and, as soon as the program came to an end, the phone rang. It was Peg. She said that I had led the way for all the best kid actors in films and that when they made me, as

From the moment Peggy and Sybil Jason met, they were instant friends.
(From the collection of Sybil Jason)

an actress, they broke the mold. Coming from THE best child actress herself in MY estimation…well…it can't get any better than that!"

In a letter to Cas, Virginia vented her frustration at the lack of meaningful communication between herself and Peggy. Cas wished she could help but, being so far away now from her grandmother, she could only offer comfort in a letter. "You should know better than to let my mom get you so depressed," she wrote. "That's just the way she is and I doubt if she will change, so just take it for what it is. I know it still hurts you very much, but you're a good and strong person and you've got to think about yourself and your own life. You'll always have a granddaughter who cares very much. Don't ever forget it either. I see you as a beautiful person and I love you very much." Virginia was indeed fortunate that she had this granddaughter. They were like lifeboats that kept each other afloat.

Peggy did try to reach her mother in March to wish her a happy birthday, but her phone call went unanswered. She then sent a telegram: "DEAREST MOTHER, HOPE YOU HAD A LOVELY DAY. ALL MY LOVE. PS: TRIED TO PHONE NO LUCK. PEGGY"

A few months later, on July 14, 1980, Peggy joined her friend Margaret O'Brien at the Academy of Motion Picture Arts and Sciences in Beverly Hills. The purpose of this event was to pay tribute to child performers of the 1930s and 1940s who had won Special Oscars. Peggy was dressed beautifully, but appeared thinner now. When the two ladies were introduced and applauded, Peggy responded, "How nice that you remember the things we did. I wish they would bring it all back." It seemed that they apparently weren't grooming child actors as well anymore because none had won the Special Oscar since 1960. "Today you're dealing with a different set of values. Youth is different today," said Peggy.

Things were starting to look a bit better. She was getting work. Small parts, perhaps, but at least casting directors still remembered her.

Peggy, together with Patty Duke Astin, Donald O'Connor, Jane Withers, Jackie Coogan, Margaret O'Brien, and Gloria Jean, were appointed by Columbia Pictures and producer Ray Stark as advisors in the search for a young actress to star in the upcoming film *Annie*. An adorable child named Aileen Quinn won the role.

Cas, too, felt that things were looking up for her mother. "Saw my mom a while ago," she wrote to Virginia. "She is doing a lot better as far as the pills go, but she is still taking them and drinking. She really seems as if she would like to make amends with you, but she is afraid to reach out to you, probably out of guilt."

The year 1981 brought some sad news. Barbara Whiting's mother, who had been like a surrogate mother to Peggy when she had needed one so badly, was gravely ill. Peggy dropped everything to be with them at this difficult time. "Peggy Ann was there and she stayed around the apartment for a long time," says Barbara. "She was right there, helping me as much as possible." Peggy was again like a part of the family, and she grieved right along with Barbara and her sister Margaret when Mrs. Whiting died.

Once she returned home, it was back to work. Peggy appeared with Cesar Romero and John Payne at a college tribute to the late producer Darryl F. Zanuck. This event was reported in the August/September 1981 issue of *Movie News*, which referred to the trio as "yesteryear favorites."

In February 1982, Peggy was invited to Elizabeth Taylor's fiftieth birthday party in London. She happily accepted, and mentioned as much to Virginia. The next month, Virginia wanted more details. In order to encourage her daughter to open up to her, Virginia promised to get her career back on top again if they could be close as they were in their early years. That was not likely to happen, however. Not only had Peggy lost her trust in her mother and the feeling of closeness long ago, but she was also realistic enough to know that Virginia no longer had any clout in Hollywood. The older woman was delusional to think she did.

This same year, a documentary was made about child actors. Entitled *Hollywood's Children*, it would be narrated by Roddy McDowall and would feature present-day interviews of some men and women who had been stars in their childhood, with footage of their early work. Now fifty years old, Peggy appeared on it briefly as she told what it was like to be a child in the razzle-dazzle world of Hollywood. Always the perfect lady, she said nothing that would be detrimental to anyone else. It was like a family on the set, she said. It was great fun and she had her own tutor. Peggy explained that a very young child, as she was at the time, doesn't freely choose to go into the business, but, rather, is put there by an adult. Once the child is grown and wants to stay in the entertainment industry, it then becomes her own decision. And that is what she did. Throughout this interview, Peggy is seen holding her beloved dog, Jake.

Her gentleman friend, Arthur Jacobson, was also given air time on this show.

Once that was done, Peggy traveled alone to Michigan to visit Barbara. This would be her last such trip.

In Twentieth Century-Fox's publication *Focus on Fox*, the June 1983 edition, was a Fox Star Retrospective article about Peggy. Entitled "Peggy Ann Garner: Oscar winner at age 13," it describes her visit once again to the Fox lot. "It's like coming home after being away for so many years," she said. "I've never had more fun than when I was a teenager on this lot back then." The studio hospital was now where her little bungalow had been. How she enjoyed reminiscing with Allan Glaser about the golden years of her youth. "I have nothing but fond memories of this place. Everyone here was so wonderful to me. It's like home."

Soon, she turned fifty-one. While there didn't seem to be much work for her, something would happen this year that would brighten her world considerably. Margaret O'Brien tells us what it was.

"Of all the projects Peggy and I worked on together—*Jane Eyre* in 1944, *I Am An American Day* in 1945, *The 50th Annual Academy Awards* in 1978, *A Tribute to Academy Oscar-Winning Child Stars* in 1980, serving on the committee together to locate the child to play the lead in *Annie* in 1980—I believe that the one that meant the most to Peggy (and me, too) was in 1983 when Peggy received the Lifetime Achievement Award. The event was at the Southern California Motion Picture Council Awards. A few years earlier, I had been the recipient of the same honor, so that wonderful group felt it would be befitting if I would come to present this award to Peggy. I agreed with great pleasure.

"This was to be an award luncheon in the Empire Ballroom at the world-famous Sportsman's Lodge in Studio City. The table where Peggy and I would be seated was in the front, very near the stage, so we wouldn't have so far to walk when we were announced by the host of this very prestigious event. The host was my very dear friend, actor Randal Malone. He was to introduce me, then I was to introduce Peggy and make the presentation to her. Just before we were to be announced, I looked over to see if she was prepared, and I saw the same look in her eyes I'd seen so many years before—a little sad. I was a bit confused and said 'Peggy, this is a wonderful event!' There were so many other stars there—Ann Miller, Ida Lupino, Bob Hope, Rose Marie, Lana Turner, just to name a few. They had all come to see Peggy get this award. She responded, 'It's not that I'm sad. I just can't believe that you and this group would be kind enough to do this for me.'

"After Randy introduced me, he turned the program over to me. I

Peggy Ann Garner on the day she received her Lifetime Achievement Award.
(Photo by Michael W. Schwibbs)

then said 'It's my great pleasure to introduce a fellow Oscar-winning child star, Miss Peggy Ann Garner. I present her this afternoon with the Lifetime Achievement Award.' She said 'This is one of the happiest moments of my career.'"

Peggy signed with the Barskin Agency, hoping they would get some acting jobs for her. Her fondest wish now was to do dinner theater or have a regular supporting role in a television series. Neither happened, but she did make an appearance on an episode of *Love Boat*. It would be her final role.

Perhaps, deep down, she knew that.

Chapter 22

Once filming was over, Peggy became very depressed and had all but cut herself off from her family. She didn't return Cas' phone calls, and sending special-occasion cards and/or flowers were the only ways she would communicate with her mother.

Depression isn't an indication of weakness, nor is it a character flaw. Rather, it's a biochemical imbalance that can tremendously affect one's body and mind. Many very creative people suffer from this disorder. Poet Rod McKuen is one of them. "When my depression took hold," he says, "I had a hard time even getting up in the morning. From the time I woke up to the time I struggled to get back to sleep it was as though there was a huge weight on my shoulders that I couldn't shake off. For months at a time I never left the house or the yard. Didn't answer mail or the telephone…My depression took me completely down. I didn't get down on others or the world but I felt so inadequate and unable to cope that I certainly didn't want to be with people."

This seems to be what Peggy was going through. Last time Cas had seen her, she was spending all day, every day, sitting in her Culver City apartment, watching television. It seemed to her daughter that Peggy had ceased to care about anyone, even herself.

This was not quite true, however. Peggy cared, but that caring, added to her financial worries, was wearing her down. In a Christmas card she sent to her mother that year, she wrote "I wish for you (and pray) just as I do for Cas and myself—We all have a healthy, happy 1984." Things might have looked bleak to her, but she knew there was always hope for a better tomorrow.

It wasn't easy to remain optimistic, either. She would love to be work-ing, but, as she told *L.A. Magazine* reporter Kathleen Newmeyer, "The producers are all so young. They say, 'Peggy Ann Garner? What does she look like?'"

"Why don't you write your autobiography?" people asked her. Peggy had no interest in doing that because she knew that what they really wanted to know was what happened to all the money she earned as a child and why her mother spent so much time in jail. Even now, Peggy didn't know the whole story about that. She was just a child at the time and hadn't understood what was happening. Of course, she had those long epistles from her mother, telling her that she had suffered much for Peggy and getting arrested was just one more act of love, but could she believe that? No, Peggy did not want to exploit their relationship in order to make a few dollars.

In the meantime, alcohol was playing a major part in Cas' life, just as it was in her mother's and grandmother's. It wasn't until now, at age twenty-seven, that Cas faced the fact that she was an alcoholic. Wanting then to do something about it, she went to some Alcoholics Anonymous meet-ings, and liked them so much that she tried to get her mother to go too. Peggy declined.

In mid-July 1984, Virginia had a serious fall in her apartment, caus-ing paralysis in both of her legs. She was hospitalized for five weeks and, with the help of physical therapy, was able to regain use of one leg.

Peggy had not been feeling very well either, but it seems to have been her mother's accident that pulled her out of her self-imposed isolation, if only briefly. "I know I'm not good at writing," Peggy wrote to Virginia, "but I'm very good at <u>feeling</u>." At that point, Peggy's concerns were in three areas. 1) She felt that it was the extreme, constant heat that was taking such a toll on her energy level. "I simply can't take heat like I used to—Getting and feeling OLD," she said. 2) It seemed that Cas' life was playing like a soap opera. She wanted to go to Reno back to "whatever his name is," Peggy wrote. "Meanwhile, 'Bobby' (her current) is losing ground. I give up. Stay tuned for the next episode." 3) It seemed to Peggy that her mother's ail-ments would be fixable if she'd only do what she was supposed to. "Please listen to the doctors, and help them take care of you," she urged.

Peggy's handwriting in this letter was much less neat than that of her previous letters, an indication that something was wrong. Virginia grew concerned. Gnawing away at her was a feeling she couldn't dispel. She

Peg's final apartment.

instinctively knew—she just felt it in her bones—that something was seriously wrong with Peggy. She tried desperately to call her, but Jacobson answered the phone and told her that Peggy wasn't there. She tried again. "I'm in the hospital," she told him, stressing that she must speak with Peggy. "I'll give her the message," he said. Another time, it seemed that someone else answered the phone—a female with a very weak voice—and softly hung up when Virginia identified herself. She wasn't even able to find Cas now, either. What was going on?

What was happening was that Peggy was dying. She had become very ill and was getting weaker every day. When she was hospitalized earlier, the doctor had diagnosed her illness as pancreatic cancer. Peggy returned to her Culver City home for a while, then went back to the Motion Picture and Television Hospital in Woodland Hills on July 25, 1984. She asked Cas not to tell Virginia she was sick. Having her around at a time like this, Peggy felt, would just make matters worse. She didn't want to have to deal with both her illness and her mother's histrionics. Cas did as Peggy requested, even though she knew that to do so would cause her grandmother to be very angry with her. But she would deal with that later.

"I visited Peggy at the Motion Picture Hospital three times a week, minimum," says Sybil Jason, "from the time she first went in for cancer til the day before she died."

Throughout the progression of Peggy's disease, Artie had been there for her as well. At the hospital, he took the room beside hers so he would be there to help however he could. "He was just sort of fatherly," said Barbara Whiting. "He was such a wonderful, warm, terrific person with her and I know she—until the day she closed her eyes—appreciated his friendship and caring."

In Artie, Peggy finally had the loving father figure she had craved all her life.

It appeared that the end was near, so Artie got on the phone and urged Barbara to come right away. Peggy needed her. She responded immediately. When Barbara walked in the door, her sick friend was so glad to see her. "We had a wonderful visit," Barbara says. She stayed for a week and spent as much time with Peggy as she could.

Once Barbara had to leave, Peggy still had Artie and Sybil nearby. Sybil recalls: "She and I shared a love of the beach and the ocean, and she wanted to have one more glance of it. A friend of mine and I got permission from her doctors to drive her down to the beach where she always experienced such peace and comfort, but the night before the trip I got a phone call where the hospital advised me that the next day would not be a good day to take her out. My vibes were not good. In fact, I went out and bought a rather large seashell that she could hold up to her ear for the time being until she was able to get down to the beach. I still have that seashell because Peg never got to see it. She died that night."

Our beloved Peggy drew her final breath on October 16, 1984, at the age of only fifty-two. Her suffering was finally over.

News traveled quickly. Newspapers all over the country notified their readers of the passing of Hollywood's beloved "Francie."

In Spokane, Washington, Peggy's second husband Albert Salmi was teaching drama classes at the Spokane Civic Theatre. One of his students broke the news to him: "At the break," says Walt Hefner, "Al and I were having a cup of coffee and I said to him, 'I was sorry to hear that your ex-wife passed away today.' Al momentarily froze and then asked, 'What are you talking about?' I told him 'Peggy Ann Garner, I thought you'd heard.' Al wanted to know how I knew this, and I informed him that it was in the local *Spokesman Review*. It was obvious that Al was very concerned, perhaps shaken, over this untimely bit of information. He informed the Gonzaga class that they were dismissed for the rest of the evening.

"My friend and I walked with Al to the parking lot where he in-

An adult Cas with her beloved Grandma. (From the collection of the DeVito family)

formed us that he didn't feel like going home yet, and would we care to join him at a nearby bar for a drink? My friend excused herself by saying she had to get home. I told Al that I'd meet him there.

"The bar was in a fairly upscale hotel and when we walked in Al wondered aloud if we could find a newspaper there. A paper was available and we sat at the bar and Al re-read the small one column by three inch article a number of times. Finally, he said, 'Poor Cas, now she's all alone. I don't know what I should do.'"

Peggy's funeral and cremation were two days later. Sybil remembers, "Peg's funeral was held in Santa Monica and, per her wishes, she was cremated and her ashes strewn on the ocean. So you see, my dear friend Peg still managed to find her final comfort at the beach." To Sybil, Peggy was "the sweetest woman on two feet!"

After saying her final goodbye to her mother at the funeral, Cas went back to Peggy's Culver City apartment. There, she found the beautiful letters that her parents had written to each other when they were a young married couple and Albert was away working on location. Peggy had kept those letters for over twenty-five years. It appears that she never stopped loving him.

Cas also discovered diaries that Peggy had faithfully kept over the years. Reading through them brought tears to her eyes. Until then, she had no idea what a difficult life her mother had had. "She suffered more than we will ever know," Cas wrote in a letter to her grandmother, "and it hurts me she couldn't confide in me." If only she had given her a chance, Cas thought, they might have been close confidantes and both their lives might have been better.

Virginia had felt the same way for years. Peggy didn't have to bear her cross alone, but chose to. She didn't want to burden others with her problems. Cas continued, "I had read not just one year's diary, but many years." She then detailed cruelties to which Peggy had been subjected from some men in her life, including one of her husbands, Kenyon. There had been some hungry years, too, when no one would help. Until now, Virginia and Cas had been unaware of that. "Now I can understand why my mom's life revolved around her little Tea Cup Yorkie, 'Jake,'" Cas said.

It was too late to have the kind of relationship Cas wanted with her mother, but she still had her faithful grandmother in Oregon. "I love you very much, Grandma," she wrote. "Please never forget or doubt that or me, okay? I'm here for you anytime and always there with you in spirit."

Cas saw her old friend, Laurie Slavin, again at a festival in Topanga Canyon. Cas' life had taken some sad turns since they were children, and it showed. "She had put on some weight, and I got the impression that things weren't going really well for her," says Laurie. "She was very happy to see me, gave me a big hug, and we talked a while. She may have had a little too much to drink that day or something because her speech was a little slurred. But she was still the same sweet person."

According to a letter Cas wrote to her grandmother, a producer approached her soon after Peggy's death. She had inherited her mother's diaries, Oscar, hardbound scripts, old *Life* magazines, Cas' baby book, pictures and letters. The producer wanted to do a tribute to Peggy, he said, and wondered if he could borrow some of these things, including her special Oscar, for this purpose. Cas, with childlike trust, complied, asking for nothing in return.

She never saw them again.

CHAPTER 23

CAS

After Peggy's death, her daughter became quite depressed. The despair lasted for about six weeks, and Cas was drinking heavily. Even when her depression had finally lifted, alcohol remained very much a part of her life, and she was consequently arrested for drunk driving. This wasn't the first time that had happened, so the punishment was thirteen days in jail and suspension of her driver's license for three years. Why was her willpower so weak, she wondered? Why couldn't she control her drinking?

Virginia, too, was having a difficult time. She was living on Social Security, and had to babysit in order to make ends meet. Nevertheless, she would send Cas money whenever she could to help with her living expenses.

It seems that Virginia had one health problem after another and tended to dramatize them to Cas in her letters. She wrote that she felt her "time is drawing near." She wanted to spend her remaining days in Ohio, and would do so as soon as the Housing Authority okayed the transfer. She did not want to die in Oregon, she said. (Her end was not as imminent as she thought, however, as she was to live ten more years after that letter was written.)

On November 12, 1985, Cas gave birth to a baby boy. She named him Christopher and wanted so badly to be a good mother to him. Her intentions were good, but the following June found Cas in jail again for drunk driving. Her son's father, Robert Calvert, and paternal grandparents took over his care.

"This place is really depressing and degrading," she wrote to her grandmother from jail. "I can't wait to get out of here. Hopefully, when I go to court Monday, the judge will let me go into an alcohol program.

The sooner I complete it, the sooner I can have my son and family back together…"

Being back with her baby was important to Cas. "I'd like to have one more child for Christopher to grow up with," she wrote. "I am missing out on so much of his growing up right now and it's really tearing me up inside. I'm reading a book on raising children from infancy to early childhood and it says from six months to one year a child really depends on his mother a lot and I'm missing all that. That's another reason why I want another child. I think two children are the perfect amount to have." Being an only child, she learned from personal experience, can be a lonely thing.

"You will be so proud of me when this is all over," she continued, "as I will be proud of myself, too. Believe me, I'm gonna do it right this time if I have the chance to do so. Say some prayers for me, okay?"

Cas could have been given a sentence up to a year, but was let off early with orders to attend Alcoholics Anonymous and parent counseling. In spite of her resolve, alcohol continued to be a problem for Cas after her release, and she was unable to provide a nurturing environment for little Chris. Consequently, the Calverts cared for him throughout his childhood. For a while, Cas stayed with them, too.

Cas' father would keep in touch, sometimes telephoning her at the Calverts'. As much as she loved her dad, she found herself hanging up on him once: Albert had been very frustrated over her situation and was sternly advising her to assume responsibility for her behavior and to shape up. Self-control was all it took, he felt, and he couldn't understand why she didn't seem to have any. Cas couldn't handle personal criticism from him and slammed the phone down.

Another hurdle for Cas to clear was her continuing unwise management of money. She worked hard and earned decent paychecks, but the money was often gone very quickly. Not only were alcohol and drugs taking a big bite out of it, but Cas meekly allowed people to take advantage of her by running up her phone bill and seeing her as a soft touch for loans that were never repaid. Her telephone had been disconnected more than once because she had been unable to pay her bill. Money was such a problem for Cas that she would sometimes live with co-workers she hardly knew, just to have a roof over her head. Her grandma scolded her for doing this, as it would surely look bad to social workers who seemed to have so much control over whether or not Cas would ever have custody of Christopher again. To Cas, though, it was a matter of either having a decent place to live or living on the streets. Grandma just didn't understand.

Virginia was unable to help Cas out much financially in the past and now it was even worse. Her income from babysitting came to a halt in July when the child she was attending was put into a State foster home. It seemed to her that Cas' father should help his daughter, and states in a 1986 letter to Cas that she felt that Roberta was behind his lack of financial support. This might have been true, as the person who managed the money in the Salmi home was, indeed, Roberta. On the other hand, Roberta might have felt that any money they would give Cas would go straight to the liquor store or drug dealer. All Virginia could do, then, was offer her granddaughter sound advice and lots of love. "Don't work in a bar or cocktail lounge," she urged Cas. "Don't tempt yourself."

Then John Carl Whiteley came into Cas' life. This mountain of a man was the answer to her prayers. "I feel so very lucky he is here and we're together because he has been my savior, because quite honestly, before I met him, I didn't care if I lived or died," she told her grandmother in a letter. "He gave me back my self and I'm sure they must have broken the mold after he was made." John was sixteen years Cas' senior, a very large man who was loving and gentle, a man of few words who had a good sense of humor and—this is surely no coincidence—was like her father in many ways. At 6'2", with blond hair, blue eyes and a gentle disposition, one could hardly come closer to duplicating Albert. Cas had so much admiration for John. "He is a master and talented in so many ways— everything he wants to learn, he will learn and be the best."

Still, how she wished she could be reunited with her father! She longingly watched him in movies, feeling grateful that he was still looking good. He and his second family had moved north to Spokane in semi-retirement, so a father-daughter reunion was no longer a simple thing to arrange. Cas felt that Roberta was always standing between them. It hurt Cas to see him so manipulated by his wife, and she was sure he was having a very difficult life.

She did have John, though. He was manager of the KOA campgrounds in Porterville, California; everyone loved him. Residents at the grounds called him "Big John, the Gentle Giant." The love Cas had for him was returned tenfold. John wanted more than anything to rescue Cas from the evil clutches the drugs had on her. He would literally cry over the damage that drugs were doing to the woman he loved. John was determined to find out who her supplier was and vowed, once he did, he would kill him.

Cas and John had two beautiful blonde-haired, blue-eyed baby girls on May 5, 1988, and September 21, 1992, but social workers felt Cas was an unfit mother and removed them from her home. The children were put up for adoption in Tulare County, California.

Cas loved children, and the loss of her daughters was agonizing to her. As her friend, Elaine, recalls: "Terry, the [KOA campground] owner, had a very soft heart, and one time this homeless family came in, and he let them live in their tent, and he also hired the dad to do some work around the campground. They were pitiful. Terry put them in a part of the campground where they would be out of sight of his customers. He just felt sorry for the kids (little girls). One night John could not find Cassie. He looked everywhere, and had decided she was off getting wasted. Now the search was really on, because he wanted to find out who she was buying her drugs from. Well, he found her. She was down at the homeless tent PLAYING with the little girls. She was having a great time. The dirt and the smell didn't seem to bother her. She went down there often, and always took the girls something—a cookie, a candy bar, or even gum. She always gave them a treat." It seems that Cas was treating those children as she was hoping other people were treating hers.

"She was a very sweet and tender woman," says Elaine. "She was very soft-spoken."

In April of 1990, Cas received the worst news of her life—her beloved father was dead. It was so sudden and unexpected, and didn't make any sense at all. Suffering from a severe case of depression, he had apparently shot Roberta, then himself. That such a sweet, gentle man as Albert would do such a thing was an utter shock, but what hurt Cas even more was knowing the agony he must have been going through that had led to such a tragic end.

"Thank God he is finally at peace," she wrote in a letter to Virginia, "even though it hurts terribly he had to suffer so many years." Cas felt such grief for the misery her father had endured for what she felt was at least two decades.

Cas went to Spokane for Albert's funeral, feeling very much like an outsider there among the people who had been close to him for so long. Thank heavens Grandma was there to console her. So grateful was Cas for Virginia's support that she bought her a card that said what was in her grieving heart: "Whatever happens to me I know I can talk it over with you…Thanks for being there!" She signed it "Love always, Cassie."

Later, she was urged by Grandma to get in touch with the Salmis' lawyer and see what provisions Albert had made in his will for Cas. She did as she was told and soon received a letter from an attorney, with a copy of her father's will. It stated that Cas had been left nothing.

"My dad did not put her in his will because I know that he figured that she would use it for something that would hurt her," says his middle daughter, Lizanne. Albert had been well aware of Cas' addiction to drugs and alcohol, and had tried time and time again to get her to quit. Knowing what damage such things could do to her had caused him much anguish.

Cas started having periods of depression in which she would isolate herself in their darkened apartment. John was her only link to the outside world at such times. It was during one of her bouts with depression that she had attempted suicide by overdosing on Dalmane. Fortunately, she was rushed to the hospital in time to save her life. Cas would usually remain in a despondent state for about a week, after which she would be back outside again, laughing and having fun with her friends as if nothing had happened.

In July of 1990, Cas made a visit to the hospital's emergency room. She was very weak, had a swollen abdomen, and there was a yellowish tint to her skin and eyes. The diagnosis was alcoholic liver with cirrhosis, and her orders were to stop drinking. How she wished that was as easy to do as it was to say.

With both of her parents now gone, Cas' relationship to her grandmother grew more intense than ever. "Grandma, you are all the family I have and I love you very much," she wrote. "I couldn't bear to lose you, especially now, and we need to spend some time together, just you and me. Ok?"

Grandma was having quite a few ailments herself by this time, which was a worry for Cas. For many years, Virginia had had severe and chronic back pain, which had been diagnosed as cervical spondylosis with mild cord compression. Her leg continued to bother her as well. Perhaps it was a result of all this that her balance was impaired. Her heavy smoking and drinking certainly did not promote glowing health, either.

Cas wrote to her grandmother often, making a valiant effort to be upbeat. Sometimes, she was too discouraged to be cheerful, though, feeling that for every step she was taking forward, she was taking several back. Virginia tried to be comforting, always remembering the birthdays of her granddaughter and her great-grandson Chris with cards. Knowing how little money Cas had, she would sometimes include some stamps or money with her letters.

Within a couple of years, Cas' cirrhosis of the liver had become complicated by premature heart disease, and her health continued to spiral downward. It was on November 8, 1993, that she gave Power of Attorney over her real and personal property to Virginia.

Cas was no longer physically able to hold a job, and she knew her time was almost up. She wanted to prepare her grandmother for the inevitable. "Souls never die," Cas wrote to Virginia. "We will be reunited again when it is meant to be. Remember, there is a reason behind everything, even if we may not understand or see the reason each time...so we must never fear death, yet welcome it with open arms and mind. Try and keep a positive mind and thoughts, because positive energy brings positive results."

Then, on Wednesday night, May 17, 1995, thirty-eight-year-old Catherine Ann Salmi left this world and went to join her mother and father. After a lifetime of yearning, they were reunited at last.

Now Virginia was alone. No more would her beloved Cas appear at her door.

The battlefield of Virginia's life was strewn with lifeless bodies—those of her two husbands, her daughter, her granddaughter—and the strong-willed matriarch was now the only one left. Had her determination to get Peggy into movies been worth it? "Be careful what you wish for—you might get it" seems to apply very much to Virginia.

It was lesson learned too late.

She grieved much for her daughter and granddaughter. Cas' philosophical words—"we must never fear death, yet welcome it with open arms and mind"—might have been on her mind when almost six months later Virginia, too, died. After decades of heavy smoking, she had succumbed to lung cancer.

In accordance with her wishes, Virginia's story is finally being told. She wanted the truth to be known. She wanted people to understand. Her mission is now accomplished.

Rest in peace, Virginia.

THE END

APPENDIX

MOTION PICTURES:

1938   *Little Miss Thoroughbred* (Warner Brothers)

1939   *In Name Only* (RKO)
    Blondie Brings Up Baby (Columbia)

1940   *Abe Lincoln in Illinois* (RKO/Max Gordon)
    (a.k.a.: *Spirit of the People)*

1942   *Eagle Squadron* (Universal)
    The Pied Piper (20th Century-Fox)

1944   *Jane Eyre* (20th Century-Fox)
    The Keys of the Kingdom (20th Century-Fox)
    The Chastitute (20th Century-Fox)

1945   *A Tree Grows in Brooklyn* (20th Century-Fox)
    Nob Hill (20th Century-Fox)
    Junior Miss (20th Century-Fox)

1946   *Home Sweet Homicide* (20th Century-Fox)

1947   *Daisy Kenyon* (20th Century-Fox)
            Thunder in the Valley (20th Century-Fox)
                    (a.k.a.: *Bob, Son of Battle)*
            Miracle on 34th Street, trailer (20th Century-Fox)

1948   *The Sign of the Ram* (Columbia)

1949   *Bomba, the Jungle Boy* (Monogram)
            The Lovable Cheat (Film Classics/Skyline)
            The Big Cat (William Moss)

1950   *Eight Witnesses* (Princess)

1951   *Teresa* (MGM)

1954   *Black Forest* (Princess)
            Black Widow (20th Century-Fox)

1966   *The Cat* (Embassy/World-Cine Associates)

1978   *Betrayal* (EMI/Roger Gimbel Productions)
            A Wedding (20th Century/Lions Gate Films)

TELEVISION:

As Regular:
1951   *Two Girls Named Smith* (Babs Smith)

As Guest:
1949   *Ford Theatre Hour* – "Little Women" (Beth March)
            The Toast of the Town (herself)
            Celebrity Time

1950   *Prudential Family Playhouse* – "Call It a Day"
            Chevrolet Tele-Theatre – "Once to Every Boy"
            Family Playhouse – "The Man"

Meet Me in St. Louis – "The Suffragettes"
After Hours Club
Hollywood Screen Test
Versatile Varieties
Leave It to the Girls

1951   Celebrity Time
Penthouse Party
The Kate Smith Hour (with husband Richard
      Hayes)

1952   Schlitz Playhouse of Stars – "Mr. Thayer"
Westinghouse Studio One – "Plan for Escape"
      (Honey Weber/Frances Westing)
Hollywood Opening Night –
      "Somebody I Know"
      "Terrible Tempered Tolliver"
The Ken Murray Show
Lux Video Theatre –
      "The Orchard"
      "Salad Days" (Judy)
Robert Montgomery Presents – "Claire Ambler"
The Kate Smith Hour – dramatic sketch "The
      Cure"
The Mel Torme Show
Twenty Questions

1953   Revlon Mirror Theatre – "A Reputation"
Suspense – "The Runaway"
Leave It to the Girls

1954   Robert Montgomery Presents –
      "Once Upon a Time"
      "From This Day Forward"
Justice – "Edge of Fear"
Twenty Questions

1955   *Stage 7* – "The Time of Day" (Miranda)
              Westinghouse Studio One – "Strange Companion"
                  (Jenny)
              Climax – "The First and the Last" (Nora Wallen)
              Best of Broadway – "Stage Door" (Kaye Hamilton)
              Robert Montgomery Presents – "Deadline"
              Danger – "Precinct Girl"
              Who Said That? (herself)
              Justice – "Shadow of Terror"

1957   *Studio One in Hollywood* – "Man Under Glass"
                  (with husband, Albert Salmi) (Katey)
              Kraft Television Theatre – "The Killer Instinct"
              DuPont Show of the Month – "Beyond This Place"
                  (Lena Anderson)

1958   *G. E. Theatre* – "The Unfamiliar" (Janey)
              Kraft Television Theatre – "The Velvet Trap"
              Sunday Showcase: Our American Heritage – "The
                  Practical Dreamer"
              The Lineup – "Thrills"

1959   *The U.S. Steel Hour* – "We Wish on the Moon"
                  (Frances Barclay)

1960   *Alcoa Presents One Step Beyond* – "Tonight at
                  12:17" (a.k.a. "The Plane Crash") (Laura
                  Perkins)
              Adventures in Paradise – "Once Around the
                  Circuit" (Deborah Baxter)
              Tate – "Stopover" (Julie)
              Dick Powell's Zane Grey Theater – "Deception" (Sarah)

1961   *Bonanza* – "The Rival" (Cameo)
              Naked City – "Button in the Haystack" (with husband,
                  Albert Salmi) (Edie Baker)

1962 *The Untouchables* – "Elegy" (Margaret Radick/
  Margaret Wilson)
 Alfred Hitchcock Presents – "Victim Four"
  (Madeline Drake)
 Adventures in Paradise – "Build My Gallows Low"
  (Lorrie Hamilton)
 Have Gun – Will Travel – "Dream Girl" (Ginger)
 Here's Hollywood

1963 *The Hallmark Hall of Fame* – "The Patriots" (Patsy
  Jefferson Randolph)
 Alcoa Premiere – "Impact of an Execution"
  (Bernice)
 The Untouchables – "The Giant Killer" (Barbara
  Sultan)
 Combat! – "Off Limits" (Nurse Lt. Amelia Marsh)
 Perry Mason – "The Case of Constant Doyle"
  (Letty Arthur)

1964 *The Man From U.N.C.L.E.* – "The Project Strigas
  Affair" (Anne Donfield)
 The Eleventh Hour – "Who Chopped Down the
  Cherry Tree?" (Myra Hopp)

1965 *The Outer Limits* – "The Probe" (Amanda Frank)

1966 *The Patty Duke Show* – "A Visit From Uncle Jed"

1967 *Batman* – "Ring Around the Riddler" (Betsy
  Boldface)

1968 *The Big Valley* – "The Prize" (Mrs. Whittaker)
 Ironside – "Price Tag: Death"

1970 *The Dating Game* (herself)

1975 *This Is the Life*

1977   *Police Woman* (probation officer)

1978   *The 50ᵗʰ Annual Academy Awards*
           Insight
           The Merv Griffin Show (herself)

1979   *Lou Grant* – "Kids" (Dixie Collins)

1980   *General Hospital*

1982   *Hollywood's Children*

1983   *The Love Boat*

RADIO:

1939   *Lux Radio Theatre* – "In Name Only"

1944   *Command Performance* – "Frankie and the Kids"

1945   *This is My Best* – "This is Violet"

1946   *Cavalcade of America* –
                   "That Powell Girl"
                   "A Little Singing, A Little Sewing"
           Screen Guild Theatre –
                   "Junior Miss"
                   "A Tree Grows in Brooklyn"
           Hollywood Star Time –
                   "A Tree Grows in Brooklyn"
                   "Junior Miss"
           The Eddie Cantor Show
           Silver Theater – "My Father and I"
           March of Dimes – Broadcast from the White House

1947   *Reader's Digest Radio Edition* – "Sunny, the Spirit
            of '76"

1948   *Family Theater* – "The World of David Lee"
            Salute to Bing Crosby
            Meet Me in St. Louis – "The Suffragettes"
            Somerset Maugham Theater – "Raw Material"

1950   *Voice of the Army* – "This Younger Generation"
            Theater Guild on the Air – "National Velvet"
            The MGM Theater of the Air – "Young Ideas"
            Hollywood Highlights – "Girl Scout Fund"

PLAYS:

1937	*Mrs. Wiggs of the Cabbage Patch*	Summer stock, Oleny theatre
1948	*The Pick-Up Girl* *Kiss and tell*	Tour
1949	*Junior Miss* *Peg O'My Heart*	Summer stock Summer stock tour
1950	*The Man*	Broadway, Fulton Theatre
1951	*The Royal Family*	Broadway, City Center Theater
1952	*First Lady*	Broadway, City Center Theater
1953	*The Youngest* *The Moon is Blue* *John Loves Mary* *Debut*	Tour Summer stock Summer stock The Empress Playhouse, St. Louis

	The Pick-up Girl	The Empress Playhouse, St. Louis
1954	*Home Is the Hero*	Broadway, Booth Theatre
	Sabrina Fair	Cincinnati Summer Theatre
	The Moon is Blue	
1955	*John Loves Mary*	Alcazar Theatre, San Francisco
	Bus Stop	National tour
1962	*Write Me a Murder*	Tour, summer circuit
	Watch the Birdie!	Tour

When the Hollywood Walk of Fame was established in 1960, Peggy was one of the first people honored with a star in this now-famous sidewalk. Her star is located at 6443 Hollywood Boulevard.

Says film and theatre critic Rex Reed, "She had turned into a fine actress with a smoky voice and probably would have ended up an important character actress in her senior years."

INDEX

231

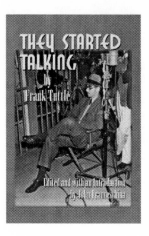

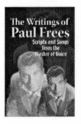

LaVergne, TN USA
04 February 2011
215168LV00001B/549/A